All Dressed Up

by Jon Marcus

CHAPTER 1

ACQUISITION

The CEO of a software company in San Francisco, Database Sparks, is speaking to all the employees in the main room of their company.

CEO: We have an announcement to make, but instead of us telling you, we thought we would let the TV news tell you.

He looks at his watch and then clicks on the televisions all over the main room.

News Anchor 1: In tech news, another Silicon Valley company has just announced their acquisition.
News Anchor 2: This acquisition is valued at 200 million dollars.

News Anchor 2: Database Sparks has been acquired by Microsoft.

The company employees all cheer. The news shows the CEO talking to a reporter while the CEO talks to the employees as waiters arrive distributing glasses of champagne to everyone.

CEO: Well done to you all. We will send an email discussing details going forward including cashing in your stock options.

The CEO turns off the televisions.

CEO: Congratulations everyone. Let the party begin.

He clicks the remote and music starts. Waiters are distributing champagne and there is a big buffet spread in the room with lots of great food and lots of booze.

A little bit later, while the party is in full swing, Norman goes outside for some fresh air. He sees some fellow employees smoking pot.

Employee: Like a hit?

Norman: No thanks.

They are passing around the joint.

Norman: Ever see a movie from 1960 called The Apartment?

Employee: No

Norman: There is a Christmas party scene, where employees were dancing, drinking and couples were making out in the offices. They just all let loose.

Employee: Sounds like days before pre-sexual harassment laws. We aren't allowed to talk about it now or even look at someone in a way they don't like.

Other Employee: No wonder people watch so much porn.

Norman: Yeah. I guess the booze they were all drinking helped get them over any inhibitions. I'm going to steal some office supplies.

Norman goes inside and into the supply closet where he is surprised to see two people are having sex. They completely ignore him. He stops and hesitates in confusion about what to do.

Norman: I just need a few things.

They continue on like he isn't even there. He grabs some pens, Post-It notes, etc and leaves. He drops the stuff at his desk and goes back to the party. As he passes the CFO's office, the CFO calls him in.

CFO: Hey Norman.

Norman: Yeah.

CFO: Sit down.

Norman: What's up?

CFO: This isn't public knowledge yet but FYI, most of that $200 million is going to the VC investors.

Norman: So I'm not retiring off of this.

CFO: No one is. And Microsoft already laid out a reorganization plan and they are cutting out half the staff....including you.

Norman: What!

CFO: Sorry man. You will still get your stock buyout but this is your last week.

Norman: Oh fuck.

CFO: I'm also going to tell you this now because you may not know it but you could have a hard time finding a job.

Norman: Hard time finding a job? What, are they trashing a recommendation?

CFO: No. Listen, I've seen this a lot. When someone gets older than 40, they experience a lot of age discrimination. It's tougher than you think.

Norman: Uh, correct me if I'm wrong but you said I helped save this company.

CFO: You did.

Norman: So what's the problem?

CFO: The problem isn't with us. We'll give you a great recommendation. But I'm telling you, this hiring crap happens a lot. And it's bullshit.

Norman: You said the young coders screwed up the code so much it almost ruined the company and the young salespeople blew deals and the young recruiters passed over good candidates.

CFO: You aren't hearing me. It's not my decision. It just happens. It's stupid, it's illegal but it happens a lot. Too much.

Pause

Norman: Why does it happen?

CFO: Because in tech the VCs actually tell us to hire young because youth is invigorating but also when potential buyers walk in the office, it makes them feel like they are in a soft core porn movie.

Norman: Are you serious?

CFO: Yes. In other industries, it's just plain old stupid. Maybe the CEOs just want to bang the young girls. I don't know. But I'm telling you, save your money.

CHAPTER 2

THE MOVE

Three months later, Norman is enjoying his unemployment. He's hanging out at cafes, biking, camping and going to concerts. He also applies to jobs regularly.

Seven months after that, Norman hasn't found a job. He realizes he has to cut expenses. The largest is rent. So he calls a few friends to ask around. They don't know of anything. Then he calls his friend Phil.

Phil: Hey Norman, I was just about to call you. My roommate just gave notice. If you know anyone looking, let me know.
Norman: How about me?
Phil: Still can't find a job?

Norman: Right. I'm going to cut back expenses and rent is at the top of the list.

Phil: OK. First of the month?

Norman: Sounds good.

He moves in on the first of the month. After all his stuff is in (and still in boxes) he lies down on the mattress and falls asleep.

Five months later, Norman still doesn't have a job.

CHAPTER 3

THE RUNNER AND THE SHRINK

The sun is rising over San Francisco as seen from the hills on the other side of the Golden Gate Bridge. People are getting coffee at coffee shops. Bakeries are getting items delivered to their stores. Fishing boats are coming in to the docks and crab kiosks are making their food on Fisherman's Wharf for future customers. People are driving down Lombard Street (the crookedest street in the world).

Norman is in his room, lifting weights. He's in good shape. When he's done he calls out to Phil.

Norman: Phil, I'm going to take your dog for a walk, ok?
Phil: Great!

Norman calls out to the dog, whose name is Pavlov.

Norman: Pavlov, want to go for a walk?

Pavlov comes over wagging his tail. He's a Rhodesian Ridgeback, a beautiful brown dog with very short hair and a ridge of slightly raised hair running down its back. They were bred in Southern Africa to assist in hunting lions.

Norman puts Pavlov on a leash, pets him and then they head out the door. A few minutes into the walk, a beautiful woman jogs by and she smiles at Norman when she runs by him.

Norman: (to the dog) That's why I walk you.

Norman walks into a coffee shop and gets a coffee. His roommate walks in.

Norman: How did you get here so soon?
Phil: I don't wander around looking for a certain jogger.

Norman: Yeah, good point. Are you heading home? Can you take Pavlov?

Phil: You just took him a few minutes ago.

Phil pauses, realizing he's being inconsiderate to Pavlov..

Phil: Oh, right. I take it she already ran by you?

Norman: Yeah, and she smiled at me.

Phil: Nice.

Norman: Man, her smile makes me feel alive.

Phil: Give me the leash.

Norman hands the leash to Phil.

Phil: Where are you going?

Norman: Headed to the shrink. Gonna vent about the job search.

Norman starts to walk off when his phone rings. The caller ID shows it's his mom.

Norman: …and my parents.

He reluctantly answers the call.

Norman: Hi mom. No I'm not moving home.

Norman's Mom: How did you know what I was going to say?

Norman: I'm psychic.

Norman's Mom: Did you find a job yet?

Norman: No.

Norman's Mom: Are you close?

Every question his mom asks is out of concern but they all revolve around the unemployment situation he's in that gives him anxiety.

Norman: Am I close? No one ever really knows if they are close to getting a job. I've had great interviews but never heard from them again. A few years ago I had what I thought was a bad interview and then a month later they called and offer me a job. One time a guy said he was sending an employment contract over but that contract never came because he ended up hiring his nephew.

Norman's Mom: So what are you going to do? I'm so worried about you.

Norman's Dad: Is that Norman? Do what your mother says!

Norman: Don't worry mom. Its all OK. I will be fine.

Norman walks over to his psychiatrist's office. His shrink is a man in his 50s who has an office in his home. The home is a typical San Francisco house with 3 stories and a multi-gabled roof. The office has a lot of wood furniture, leather chairs, a leather couch and looks out over a back yard with many trees.

Norman: Doc, I'm in trouble.

Dr. Allen: What's up.

Norman: I am so stressed out. I've been out of work for nearly two years, money is getting tight and my mom won't stop asking me to move home.

Dr. Allen: Is that an option you want to consider?

Norman: That's all I need. I'll just move back into my childhood bedroom with the Star Wars posters on the walls and disappear into oblivion. It's not just moving back home, it's moving back in time.

Dr. Allen: And how does that make you feel?

Norman gives him a mean look.

Norman: Really? (pause) How does that make me feel? I told you. It's stressing me out! I'm trying to keep my wits about me. I don't need my mother's micromanagement of my life like I'm a child. Not to mention my dad will just keep pushing me and not even productively. He thinks applying pressure in any direction is helping. Between the two of them, it's like living in an insane asylum. Which by the way, I'm heading towards if something doesn't work out soon. I bet half the crazy homeless people out there ended up there because they just couldn't find a job.

Dr. Allen: So what are you going to do?

Norman puts his hands over his face.

Norman: I don't know.
Dr. Allen: OK Norman. Take a deep breath. You are in a safe place here. Try to relax for a moment.

Norman takes a deep breath.

Dr. Allen: Is that better?

Norman: No

Dr. Allen: There is a good concept that helps people in times of stress. Take it one day at a time.

Norman: One day at a time.

Dr. Allen: Yes. Many times people start thinking ahead so much that it gets in the way. But things can change in an instant in any direction and that's life. Live in the present.

Norman: Live in the present.

Dr. Allen: Right. The future doesn't exist yet. Sure we try to do things that will send us on good paths and avoid pitfalls, but we only live in the present. You do the best you can and you take it one day at a time.

Norman: One day at a time.

Dr. Allen: Don't run through life trying to catch the future. You don't live there and you can't catch the future. Slow down and take time to smell the roses. And when you do, an option might present itself that fits in and you wouldn't have noticed if you were running past it.

Norman still has his hands on his face.

CHAPTER 4

A PLEA FOR HELP

Norman and some friends are seated at a table at a nice restaurant. There is soft music in the background.

Norman: OK everyone, thanks for showing up.
Lois: How could we refuse a free dinner?
Norman: Did I say free?

They all laugh. Stan gets up with a smile on his face.

Stan: Let's go.

They all look at him. He, and everyone, knows Norman is in trouble so he sits back down.

Norman: I've gathered you all here today because...I have a problem and I need the greatest minds in the universe to help solve it.

Greg: So why did you invite us?

They laugh.

Norman: OK, the greatest minds and Greg.

They laugh again.

Fanny: Let's hear it.

Norman: My job search has gone on too long.

Stan: Yup.

Lois: Oh that.

Jim: Uh huh.

Fanny: Yes.

Greg: We know.

Patricia: Yep.

Norman: Nothing is working. I need ideas and I need them now. I'm asking for brainstorming. No idea is dumb. Say whatever comes to mind.

Stan: OK. Let's order some wine.

Stan hails the waiter. Norm can tell already that this isn't going to go well.

Norman: Whatever comes to mind <u>about my job search.</u>

Stan hails the waiter, who comes over.

Waiter: Yes sir.
Stan: Can we get a bottle of Zinfandel, a bottle of Chardonnay and a bottle of Merlot?

Then Stan asks the people at the table.

Stan: Anything else?
Lois: No.
Jim: Nope.
Fanny: Uh, no.
Greg: That'll do it.
Patricia: All good.

Ten minutes later, the waiter has left the wine, the people have their wine of choice in their glasses and they all start drinking. Norman just has water. He doesn't drink.

Stan: To Norman.
All: To Norman:

They all take a drink.

Norman: Thanks everyone, but I need a job.
Patricia: OK, if you really need money, have you looked for temp work?
Norman: They just hire women.
Lois: Boooooo.
Patricia: Oh come on.
Fanny: Yeah right.
Norman: No it's true. I tried a number of agencies and always got BS excuses like they only wanted people with previous job titles of Admin Assistant or Office Manager or they just aren't busy and don't need more candidates.
Lois: What's wrong with that?
Norman: Then I called someone I know back east who runs a temp agency and she told me their clients all ask for women and the owners of the agency won't

tell the clients to fuck off because it happens so often they wouldn't have any clients.

Jim: How about gig jobs?

Norman: No. I've talked to enough people that have done them. Just no.

Fanny: Are you on unemployment?

Norman: I'm on it. It helps but it's not enough to live on. It's not even enough to pay rent. Plus mine is running out.

Lois: Can you move home?

Norman: I'll kill myself… or my parents… or both.

Greg: How about prostitution?

Norman: I may be wrong but I don't think women will pay for my services.

Jim: Who said anything about women?

They all laugh.

Patricia: Why don't you take any job you can find. Just to get some income.

Norman: I ran the numbers. The thing is that I can't afford rent and expenses on low wage jobs.

Fanny: Yeah, wages have definitely not kept up with inflation.

Lois: Have you tried investing in lottery tickets?

Norman: I am trying but for some reason it isn't working.

Jim: What if you lowered your expectations and took a job you can survive on or that is a pay cut but you can get by on?

Norman: I am trying to apply for lower level jobs but I think they see me as overqualified and assume I will leave in a few months when I find a better job. As for jobs I've never done before, if I can't get a job with 20 years of experience, how am I going to get one with zero experience?

Patricia: Have you tried government jobs?

Norman: Yes and surprisingly if you don't have really specific skills, the only thing left are low wage jobs that don't pay the bills. Even forest ranger jobs, which I would love, require experience.

Greg: How much are you networking?

Norman: A lot. I'm even resorting to taking friends to dinner.

Jim: Getting nowhere, huh?

Norman: Apparently employers prefer the allure of a peppy person who does whatever bad idea they tell them to do and gets drunk with them after work...or anything else after work. Their hiring practices are like electing politicians. They both are hired more on charisma and fairy tales than on competence and track records.

Patricia: Elections should be job interviews, not the desire to hang out and drink with your pal. The same thing is happening in the workplace.

Jim: What amazes me is companies complain that they can't find good employees and then they lobby congress to open up hiring from other countries when in fact they can hire from here but they would have to hire people over 30 and they don't want to. They set up their companies like its a party club.

Fanny: Maybe Greg is right?

Norman: About what?

Fanny: Prostitution.

Norman: Getting back to my job search...I need contacts. Who do you know?

They all sit there thinking silently. Norman and the others talk it out while they eat and drink. Norman is just drinking water. Nothing comes of his attempt to prod them for ideas or contacts. Eventually they split the bill and get up to leave..

Jim: Do you need a ride home?

Norman: No thanks. I'm just going to hang out here.

Jim: But you don't drink.

Norman: I know. I just feel like thinking and being around happy strangers. I just want to stop and smell the roses.

Jim: OK. Talk to you soon.

Greg: See you buddy.

Greg gives him a manly hug.

Norman: Greg always with the hugs.

Greg: Let me know if I can help.

Norman: Thanks.

Greg: See you Jim.

Greg gives Jim a hug too.

Fanny: Good night Norman.

Norman: Bye.

The others are already out the door.

Norman: (To the bartender) Can I get a water?

Bartender: One water.

Norman: Thanks.

Norman tips him a dollar.

Bartender: Thank you.

A beautiful woman in a classy and sexy black dress comes over, stands very close to Norman and orders a drink.

Marianne: Can I get a cabernet? (She looks at Norman). What's the matter pumpkin?

Norman: Oh, you know. This and that.

Marianne: I've been there. Is that a giant glass of vodka or gin or water?

Norman: Just water.

Marianne: What's the story here?

Norman: About the water?

Marianne: Sure let's start there.

Norman: I just don't like myself when I drink. I don't like acting stupid. I don't like saying stupid things. I don't like gaining weight. At some point I said, why am

I doing this? Because everyone else does? Because it looks sophisticated?

Marianne: Good point.

Norman: I felt like I had succumbed to pier pressure like I was a little kid being pressured by the other kids. So I stopped.

Marianne: You like making speeches don't you?

Norman: A little bit.

She puts her hand out.

Marianne: Marianne.

He shakes her hand.

Norman: Norman.

There is a moment as they don't let go of each others' hands.

Norman: So what are you up to tonight?

Marianne: Oh, my friend just left.

Norman: Same here. How was your meal?

Marianne: I didn't eat here. A girlfriend and I went to a concert. We just felt like grabbing a drink afterwards.

Norman: We?

Marianne: She got a text from her husband and went home.

Norman: Oh. What concert?

Marianne: It was a Spanish guitarist.

Norman: Nice.

Marianne: Actually, I don't know why I got this wine. I have a big day tomorrow.

Norman: Slaying dragons?

Marianne: Yes. You'd be surprised how many dragons there are out there. And they multiply like bunnies.

Norman: Oh, yes. Bunny dragons.

Norman is an engineer and conversing with women is not his forte. In fact he is terrible at it. But he likes her. The bartender however is listening to this conversation, feeling sick and shaking his head "no."

Marianne: Yeah. You think there is just one sleeping in a cave somewhere. But when you go to hunt it down and it has a whole family and a bunch of horrible friends.

Norman: Its like a gang.

Marianne: A gang indeed. They are all over the place. How about you? Do you also hunt dragons? Are you here contemplating storming the castle soon?

Norman: No, I don't storm castles. I get other people to do that.

Marianne: Smart.

The bartender coughs hoping to interrupt and stop the conversation.

Norman: Meanwhile I sit back and listen to the minstrels play.

Marianne: Ooo. That sounds like a great life.

Norman: I'm working on it.

Marianne: Well, if it gets too dull, you are welcome to join me and my crew on a dragon hunt.

Norman: I will keep that in mind.

Marianne: Well, its getting late and this dragon metaphor is getting old.

Bartender: Indeed it is.

Marianne: I should probably be going.

Norman: Me too. Let me walk you out.

Marianne: That would be nice. Let me order a ride home first.

Norman: (to the bartender) Here's another 5 for the inflicted trauma.

Bartender: Thanks.

She is tapping on her phone and he is looking at her. Eventually she sets it up, lowers the phone and takes one last sip finishing off her wine.

Norman: Marianne... can I call you?

Marianne: Yes. Enter your number in my address book.

She hands Norman her phone and he types his number in.

Marianne: And…

Then she calls him. His phone rings and she hangs up.

Marianne: Now you have my number too.

He smiles at her. They walk outside and her ride shows up. She checks the license plate to make sure its hers.

Marianne: This is mine.

Norman: OK

He opens the door for her. She gives him a hug, gets in the car and leaves. As Norman starts to walk home, a transvestite walks by him. He turns, looks and then walks away in the other direction.

CHAPTER 5

APPLICATIONS

The next day, late morning, Norman wants to see his beautiful, jogging, fantasy girlfriend.

Norman: Here Pavlov. Let's go get some coffee.

Pavlov comes running. Norman put the leash on him and takes Pavlov for a walk. At one point a few blocks away, he sees across the street, the beautiful runner. She smiles at him again. He smiles back and waves. She runs off and he goes to the coffee shop, gets a coffee and goes home. His roommate has something to say to him.

Phil: Dude.

Norman: What.

Phil: You were gone 9 minutes. I don't mind letting you use my dog to try to meet this woman, but at least take him for a real walk.

Norman: Yeah. That's fair.

He turns around and takes Pavlov out again.

Norman: Let's go look at the water Pavlov.

Norman takes Pavlov for a long walk which goes down the very steep hills in Pacific Heights to the Marina district and then to the waters edge at Marina Green.

He finds a bench overlooking the San Francisco Bay and and sits on the end so Pavlov can rest next to him. Lots of expensive boats are tied to the docks nearby. Alcatraz is to the right. The Golden Gate Bridge is to the left and half fogged in. The rest of the sky is clear and blue. You can hear fog horns. Norman starts searching the internet on his phone and talks to Pavlov.

Norman: Pavlov. I'm going to apply to some jobs. I've already applied to a thousand of these, but I'm sure this time it will be different. I wonder what thrills await me on job websites.

He fishes around job websites on his phone.

Norman: This looks interesting. Let's press Apply. Yes, I agree to your terms. No, I'm not going to read the 25 pages of your terms. I hope you aren't selling my information all around the world, but you probably are. Pavlov, why doesn't Congress make strict privacy laws? Please upload resume. OK.

He uploads his resume and fills out the information they ask for - email address, phone number, location, etc.

Norman: OK, screening questions.

An older African-American woman sits down in the middle of the bench near he is on.

Norman: Are you 18 or older? Yes. Why are you interested in our company? Ugh, I hate these stupid questions. Did they hire a high school student to put these in here? (He types) "Because you have a great product and the company is going somewhere." Assholes. What accomplishment are you most proud of? (He types) "I am most proud of filling out this application." I may not get this job Pavlov.

Older Woman: Ha.

Norman looks at her as he realizes she couldn't help but hear him talking.

Norman: Sorry.
Older Woman: That's OK. Besides, I'm sure your dog is learning something.

He smiles at her joke and goes back to the application.

Norman: Please provide the following voluntary information. Gender. There's a red asterisk there. Look Pavlov. (he shows the phone to Pavlov) They make you respond to the voluntary identification questions. Decline to self identify. Race. Decline to self identify. Veteran Status. Decline to self identify. Sexual orientation. What are you fucking kidding me? I wonder if the companies use these responses to pick which candidates they want to talk to.

An older white man sits down next to the older woman. They are friends.

Older Woman: (to her friend) Listen to this (she points at Norman).
Norman: Decline to self identify. Are you of Latin origin? Why is that a separate category from race? Decline to self identify. I can't decline? I have to answer the Latin question? Oh, these people suck.

The older people laugh softly.

Norman: Disability Status? This includes... geeze this is a long list. Hmmmm. Kiss my ass is not an option here. I guess, Pavlov, they think discrimination is ok as long as its against white men. Decline to self identify. They don't ask my age. Submit. Maybe I should break down and just start drinking.

The older woman laughs.

Norman: Where else can I apply?

Older Man: Job search frustrating you?

Norman: It's the economy.

Older Woman: No it's not.

Norman: Excuse me?

Older Man: Past your 30s?

Norman: A little.

Older Woman: Figure it out?

Norman: What are you talking about?

Older Woman: Let me guess. You have all this great experience, but it's getting harder to find a job.

Norman: Yeah, how did you know?

Older Man: And the companies hire cute smiling idiots who don't know what they are doing?

Norman: Actually, I'm starting to notice that.

Older Man: Yes. It's something illegal that no one talks about in our society.

Norman: Illegal?

Older Woman: It's called age discrimination.

Norman: I'm not old.

Older Man: Don't worry, it happens to everyone.

Older Woman: Forced retirement. Posting jobs for people with 2 years experience.

Older Man: All the games company employees play to avoid hiring people they don't want to go drinking with or have sex with.

Norman: I'm not old.

Older Woman: Neither are we.

The man and woman eventually leave. Norman sits there for hours thinking of what those two people said. In that time many people walk by; some sit and feed the pigeons. Sail boats go in and out of the marina where they were docked and a few large cargo ships go under the Golden Gate Bridge into the SF Bay headed to the ship yards in Oakland. Norman just sits there and thinks and wonders if those two people were right and his job search and money problems are due to age discrimination?

CHAPTER 6

JUJITSU

Marianne is leading a Jujitsu class. She is a black belt and the instructor. She is throwing people, getting thrown and when she gets thrown, she knows how to roll out of it so she doesn't get hurt. She teaches those skills to the others in the class. They not only practice throws and rolls, they practice attacks.

As a demonstration to the class, there is one particularly large guy who comes at her and she throws him across the room. She is smaller than him but knows how to use an attacker's momentum and body position against them. The size of the guy doesn't matter. She is fierce.

You would never know by looking at her anywhere else that she has a black belt in a martial art. She is not tall or mean looking or muscular like an Amazon. The interesting thing people learn as a side effect of taking martial arts is you never assume you can overpower anyone based on their looks. Never assume a fat slob or a skinny old guy with gray hair or even an attractive woman who looks cute and effeminate in a black dress, can't kick your ass. Never underestimate anyone.

CHAPTER 7

HR

At a tech company office, the HR Director, Pete, is training a new and young person, Heather, on how to do interviews.

Pete: OK, Heather. We prefer behavioral interviews here.

Heather: What's that?

Pete: You ask open ended questions. Not anything they can respond yes or no to.

Heather: Oh.

Pete: It makes them give us detail in their answers which helps us see what they know. It can really wear them out though, but such is life.

Heather: OK. How do I do that?

Pete: I have a list of questions here. Just go through them and get the person talking.

Heather: I will have their resume and application?

Pete: Right.

Heather opens an application and looks at it.

Heather: Oh, this one didn't put their college graduation date? Should I ask?

Pete: Absolutely not. We aren't allowed to ask certain things like marital status, race, age and a few others. Asking a college graduation date can be construed as asking their age and we could get sued.

Heather: Oh.

Pete: In fact, some places require a graduation date in their online application and that is a really bad move. They are setting themselves up for trouble.

Heather: Huh.

Pete: In the beginning of the interview, just start with some pleasantries like the weather.

Heather: The weather?

Pete: Just something to be nice and loosen things up.

Heather: OK.

Pete: And then ask the questions I gave you.

Heather: Alright.

Pete: We'll have you call a few people to start.

Pete randomly picks out an application of the many in the system. It's Norman's.

Pete: Uh...here, this guy looks good. Send him an email and use this template for a phone interview.

Pete shows her where the templates are saved and he sets up the email for her.

Heather: Oh. OK.

Heather sends off the email.

Meanwhile, Norman is still sitting on a bench at Marina Green. It's nearing sunset and the fog is coming in from the ocean through the Golden Gate Bridge. Norman checks his phone and continues talking to Pavlov. Some emails that came in since he had been applying for jobs.

Norman: Oh look Pavlov. I got a few emails. Oh, I liked this company. What did they say? "Dear Norman, Regarding your application. Thanks so much for applying to our company. We are impressed with your resume, however we have decided not to continue with your candidacy..." Oh Fuck You!!! Yeah you are so impressed you decided not to even interview me? Isn't that insulting Pavlov?

Pavlov has more important things in mind. He is staring at the seagulls with the intent to run after them.

Norman: Next email. Dear Norman, Thanks so much for applying to our company. Although your resume is quite impressive...Delete.

Why do they send those depressing emails out? Assholes. Why don't they just say "Dear Norman. Your resume sucks. And besides, we want to hire someone to party with. Even though you seem to know what you are doing, forget it." No, I'm not bitter. Oh, another email just came in.

Norman opens the email.

Norman: "Dear Norman, we received your resume and would like to speak with you about a position here." …Yes!!!

He says it so loud that people for a good distance in the area turn to look. Norman sees some of them looking at him. He takes Pavlov's leash, gets up and starts to walk home. Just then, Pavlov starts pulling the other way to try to catch a seagull.

CHAPTER 8

GAME NIGHT

Norman finally gets home with Pavlov. 16 people are there playing games on four card tables they have set up. Norman knows them as they are friends' of Phil and have regular game nights there. One table is playing Risk. One is playing Scrabble, One is playing card games and one is playing Candy Land.

Phil: There you are.

Norman: You were worried about me?

Phil: No, about Pavlov. Were you out all day because you finally hooked up with that runner?

Norman: I wish. Wow, I haven't seen Candy Land since I was a kid.

Sally: It's very challenging.

Phil: So what were you doing all day?

Norman: I sat at Marina Green applying for jobs and contemplating life.

Alex: Sounds fascinating.

Norman: Oh, and I got an interview!

They all cheer and congratulate Norman.

Norman: Thanks

Phil: Who is the interview with?

Norman: Actually, I'm not sure. I don't even remember applying to them. Everything is a blur. I've got some research to do.

Sally: I would say so.

Norman: Something interesting happened today. I talked to these people who said my job search problems were because I was experiencing age discrimination.

Everyone moans.

Norman: You know about this subject?

Alex: Oh yeah. It's huge in the tech industry.

Alison: Actually it exists in every industry but especially in tech.

Norman: Huh. But I'm only 41.

Sean: Anything past 29 is old in their eyes.

Sally: And people look for it in resumes.

Norman: Excuse me?

Sean: Yeah. It's total bullshit, but they do.

Sally: The companies make their whole staff young and then complain they can't find qualified workers.

Alex: And then they lobby Congress to let them bring in people from other countries because there is such a (he uses finger quotes) "shortage."

Phil: My last company went under because even though they had good venture capital money, and a good idea, they hired so many young people, it slowed down the growth of building the product because engineering became mired down. The coders in our department just couldn't work as well. And of course then sales couldn't sell it well.

Alex: I work in recruiting and I can tell you we get hiring managers insisting on keeping the candidates young. It's totally illegal. I politely tell them to piss off but the young recruiters don't know their jobs so they will do whatever stupid things they're told. Plus the young recruiters reject great resumes and stuff.

Sean: I hate recruiters

Alex: Yeah, everyone does until they need a job.

Sean: So what's your point?

Alex: My point is fuck you.

Sean: Fuck you?

Alex: Hey asshole, you have a great job with great pay at company you didn't even know about until I called you and then sent them your resume.

Sean: Yeah well.

Alex: Yeah well. As I was saying, recruiters have to work on some sort of commission for 5 years to really learn how to do recruiting well. Once you lose a couple big commissions, you learn. Big company experience over all your career doesn't mean shit in recruiting.

Alison: I work in sales and it's the same thing there.

Larry: Book smarts isn't enough. It takes time to learn how to do one's job.

Sally: At a startup, where it's extremely competitive and there is a race against time to make the company work, weighting the staff highly to young people is the stupidest thing they can do.

Alex: I love how they say attitude is more important than experience.

Larry: Yeah. The only people who say that are ones who lack experience.

Phil: Is this a phone interview or a Zoom interview?

Norman: Phone. Why?

Phil: I have an app… well a Zoom browser extension that makes you look younger. It changes any gray hair to your regular color and it smoothes over wrinkles.

Alison: Funny.

Sean: What's the browser extension called? I'll look it up.

Phil: Face Lift.

CHAPTER 9

THE PHONE INTERVIEW

Norman goes to a coffee shop, sits down and researches the company. He takes his time finding out what they do, who runs it, any articles about them including product news and financing news.

After a few hours, Norman feels like he needs to clear his brain. He heads home sits no the couch and watches a movie. Then he watches another movie and falls asleep on the couch.

The next morning he wakes up and goes for a walk. In San Francisco, a walk is exercise thanks to the hills and he knows a set of stairs a few blocks away that go up and down a few very long and steep blocks. The stairs have a great view and many people go there to exercise. Norm and others go walking up and down stairs.

After an hour he has had enough and he walks back home, eats breakfast and takes a shower. Then he does a little more research on the company as his phone interview is later that day.

Later, Norman is exercising in his room to loud music. Then he turns off the music, goes to the kitchen and grabs an apple from the fridge. Phil tis there.

Norman: Phil, I am pumped for this phone interview. I read up on this company and I am going to nail this thing.
Phil: Excellent. Go get 'em.

Norman looks at a clock. Its 1:30 pm.

In the company offices:

Pete: OK, Heather. You have your questions ready?
Heather: Yes.

Pete: Now this guy has a lot of experience, but he's a little old so we aren't going to hire him so don't be nervous. It's just practice. I'll be here.

Heather: Old. Isn't that age discrimination?

Pete gives her the evil eye.

Pete: Just call him. If he sounds ok, we can even invite him in for an in-person interview and you can get a practice round for that too.

Heather: OK.

She dials the number.

Norman: This is Norman.

Heather: Hi Norman. This is Heather calling to talk about the job here. Is this still a good time to talk?

Norman: Yes it is Heather. Let's talk.

Heather: All right. You sound rarin' to go.

Norman: It's a great day to be alive.

Heather: First, I'll tell you about what we do and then we can talk about your background.

Norman: Sounds good.

Heather: We are an aerospace startup. We are developing software for satellites. We got our start a few years ago when our founder left NASA to start his own company. So far we have raised 75 million dollars in venture capital and we are expanding. So I see you are a database engineer. And, Oh, you have a Masters degree in it from Stanford.

Norman recognized that "Oh" meant she was surprised at the Masters degree so she hadn't read his resume. That means either she is not good at her job or she showed her hand that she doesn't intend on hiring him. He'll have to play along and see what happens.

Norman: Yes. In fact I worked on some data transmission devices that were used for telecom data towers which I think would lend itself well to what you folks are doing there.

Heather's boss is watching and pointing to questions.

Heather: Great. Tell me about a time you were proud of an accomplishment at work.

We hear **Norman's internal dialog**:

"Proud of an accomplishment? Standard behavioral question. She is young and new at this. An older person wouldn't ask such a general bullshit question. So if she wants to bullshit me, I will bullshit her back."

Norman: To be honest, I take great pride in my work and I make sure every day is an accomplishment. In my last company...

In the theme of bullshit, Norman gives a lengthy reply to this question. Heather isn't even listening. She is paying attention to hand signals her boss is giving about what to do next. When Norman stops talking, there is a pause until Heather realizes he stopped talking. Then she asks her next question.

Heather: Tell me about a time when you disagreed with your boss. And what happened?
Norman: Disagree with my boss? Actually I was fortunate to have some really great managers...

Norman gives a lengthy praise of his former managers and relays a random example of a slight disagreement he and the rest of the engineering staff debated on a subject and then resolved to everyone's satisfaction.

Heather: Describe a situation where you and a coworker were in conflict.
Norman's internal dialog: *"Geeze, this is grueling. These people are hard core on the behavioral stuff."*

Norman: OK. Well people disagree all the time. One time though...

Norman looks at the clock and its 2:10pm. Heather has been asking him these tough questions for almost 45 minutes. Norman is worn out.

Heather: Well, this was very educational.

Pete points to words on a page that say "Invite him in for an interview?" The boss gives her a thumbs up.

Heather: Can you come in and meet a few people for an interview?

Norman: Absolutely!

Heather: Great. I'll email you some scheduling options. Thank you for your time. Have a nice day.

Norman: Thanks. You too.

They all hang up.

Pete: That was good. These questions are made to be tough and I've literally seen mature grown ups sweat and even cry when being hit with them and overwhelmed in an interview.

Back at Norman's apartment. Norman's door is open and he is slouched in his chair looking tired. Phil walks over and stands in the doorway.

Phil: Are you sweating?

Norman is in fact sweating. He looks at Phil like he just ran a marathon. He nods his head yes.

Norman: That was the most brutal interview I've ever had. It's like they wanted to break me.

Afterwards, Norman goes into the kitchen and makes a sandwich.

Norman: I am going to get this job.
Phil: That's the attitude!
Norman: Oh it's not attitude. I am going to make them hire me.
Phil: How can you <u>make</u> them hire you?
Norman: They want to play hardball with me. I will play hardball with them.
Phil: What are you talking about? What are you going to do?
Norman: I am going to that in-person interview in a dress!
Phil: What?
Norman: Yup, I need a dress. Want to go with me to a dress store?
Phil: Are you fucking kidding me?

Norman: I'm serious. Let's go.

Phil: I thought you were trying to get this job.

Norman: I am.

Phil: Then what's with the dress?

Norman: It's for protection.

Phil: Dude, I'm getting close to calling the psych ward. What is going on?

Norman: There are discrimination laws. They all find sneaky ways to get around the age stuff but they wont be able to get around the gender stuff..

Phil: Oh man. Norman, you are talking about wearing a dress to a job interview!

Norman: Yeah. When they see the dress, they will forget wondering about my age.

Phil: I think the stress from being unemployed is getting to you.

Norman: I think I'm thinking more clearly than ever before. So are you going to help me pick out a dress?

Phil: Not in a million years.

CHAPTER 10

NORMAN'S FIRST DRESS

Norman goes to a small dress store he's seen in Noe Valley a few times.

Eve: Can I help you?

Norman: Yes, I need a dress.

Eve: <u>You</u> do?

Norman: Yes, well, its a birthday present for my sister.

Eve: Oh, what kind of dress?

Norman: I don't know, Something I could - she could wear to an interview.

Eve: We have these business suits. Or maybe even a nice sundress. What kind of company?

Norman: Its a tech company.

Eve: Oh, you can wear anything to them. But everyone there dresses casually. So let's go with a sundress.

Norman: Yes. Let's.

Eve: You like this?

Norman: It's very nice.

Eve: Or how about this?

Norman: I like that one too.

Eve: What size is she?

Norman: She's about my size. We are fraternal twins.

Eve: Oh.

Norman: Any chance I could try them on?

Eve: You want to try them on?

Norman: Sure. It's San Francisco. Why not?

Eve: Well, no one else is in the store. OK. The dressing rooms are back there.

Norman: Thanks.

Eve: Do you want to buy a slip or anything?

Norman: No Thanks. Unless you think I should.

Norman tries a few dresses on and upon asking, Eve gives her opinion. He picks a few out, pays for them and goes home.

On the bus, he is noticing what women are wearing, more than he ever noticed. When he gets home, he puts on a dress and walks over to Phil's room. Their dog sees Norman and looks confused.

Norman: What do you think?

Phil: You are really doing this?

Norman: Yeah man. Hey, I haven't had an in-person interview in a long time. This could be the last one I ever have.

Phil: You got that right.

Norman: It has to be done. I basically don't have a choice.

Phil: Your only choice is to wear a dress?

Norman: Yes. I already explained it to you. Ya know, I should take it for a test run.

Phil: What do you mean?

Norman: I want to be comfortable in the interview and if I've never worn this in public, who knows what will happen.

Phil: Yeah, who knows.

Norman: I'll take Pavlov for a walk. Here Pavlov!

Pavlov comes out from the back room, looks at Norman and runs away.

Phil: No 3 minute walks. If you take him, it has to be for at least 20 minutes.

Norman chases after Pavlov. In the process, he catches the dress on a doorknob and also trips on the dress. Then he catches Pavlov, puts the leash on him and tries to take him for a walk, but Pavlov is resisting, digging his heels in. Eventually he drags Pavlov out the front door into the building lobby and Pavlov loosens up. As he is about to walk out the building front door, the beautiful runner runs by his building.

Norman: Oh, thank god she didn't notice me.

He waits a minute, opens the door and carefully looks around to see if she is close by. He doesn't see her. Generally, he only sees her once each time so he feels he is safe. He walks out the door with Pavlov and walks down the street. A few neighbors that see him give him weird looks. One holds in a chuckle when he passes Norman. At one point, Pavlov poops and Norman has to lean over and pick up the poop with a plastic bag. He looks awkward doing this in a dress. Norman doesn't want to risk encountering the beautiful runner so he goes home soon. He feels relieved when he's safe inside the building and safer in his apartment.

Phil: How was the test run?

Norman: Interesting. You know, San Franciscans aren't as open minded as they claim to be.

Phil: Oh?

Norman: Well, I guess they left me alone and that's the best I could ask for. But I'll be honest, I'm not looking forward to taking the bus to the interview.

Phil: Dude, the bus is not going to be the problem.

Norman: What do you mean?

Phil: San Francisco is a small town. You could run into people you know. Also, if you get the job and wear normal clothes when not at work, you could run into co-workers who might think you are scamming the company. More importantly, some people in this world are crazy and when you are wearing the dress, maybe you should carry pepper mace in your purse.

Norman: Purse. Oh right. This thing doesn't have pockets. Geeze. Dressing like a woman is complicated.

Norman puts on his regular clothes and goes to a store to buy a purse.

At the store, he goes up to someone who works there.

Norman: Hi. Do you have a nice purse that would go with a cheery sundress?

CHAPTER 11

NORMAN'S FRIENDS

Norman's friends from dinner the other night, meet to discuss what they might do for Norman. The doorbell rings and Greg opens the door.

Greg: Hi Lois, Jim. (He hugs them both). Glad you could make it. Stan and Patricia just got here.

Lois: Good to see you.

Jim: Thanks for organizing this.

Greg: Thank Fanny. It was her idea.

Lois: Hi everyone.

Fanny: Hi guys, come on in. Can I get you anything to drink?

Jim: No, I'm good.

Lois: You are having wine; I'll have wine.

Patricia: Hi. Nice to see you both.

Lois: You too.

Stan: OK, the subject of the night; what's everyone thinking about Norman's situation? What can we do?

Fanny: I don't know. The poor guy. He's trying so hard to find something.

Jim: I keep thinking of people I can call on his behalf but I don't work with engineers.

Patricia: Who says it has to be engineers?

Jim: Well, Norman's an engineer.

Lois: I think what Patricia means honey, is maybe we know people who work at tech companies in any department but who might be able to help Norman. You know like in sales or HR, but they can refer him to their engineering people. Do we know any HR people?

Greg: Not me. I try to avoid HR people.

All: Yeah, right, me too.

Jim: I work in health insurance so there isn't a lot of crossover there. I'm not networked with those people.

Greg: I try to avoid health insurance people too. Talk about a sleazy industry. (Greg gets a mean look from Jim) No offense.

Jim: No, of course not. Actually... you're right.

Stan: Fanny, you work in solar. That's kind of tech. Do you know anyone?

Fanny: Well, I work with a solar panel installer. So we are more in the construction field. But I can ask the owner and some people there. Maybe they have a contact.

Lois: How about you Stan?

Stan: Non-profit. Not really my thing. You know though, one of my co- workers was talking about her brother who is a systems administrator. Maybe he knows someone. I'll ask her.

Jim: How about you Greg?

Greg: I've been thinking. No one comes to mind yet.

Lois: And I work at a small company. I would say he could apply for something but we aren't hiring.

Patricia: Yes, but what about outside your company.

Lois: I don't know anyone who is hiring.

Fanny: Of course you don't. Its not like our friends call us any time a job opens up in their company. But there's always hiring going on. I guess the thing is to just help him meet other people and maybe one of them might know of something.

Stan: You never know.

Fanny: Right. Just keep the conversations going. Eventually something might happen. It's really easy to pick up the phone and ask a few people you know if they know of anything

Jim: Yes. Actually, now that I look at it that way, there are a few people I could see if they are open to an introduction. A guy at work who is in marketing, I think his prior job was in tech, and a few people from my last two jobs.

Fanny: Oh, that is just great.

Greg: Hey, I've got a few tickets to the Giants game next week. Anyone want to go?

Stan: Ooo yeah. I'll go.

Jim: Me too.

Lois: I'm really worried about Norman. I just hope he doesn't do anything stupid.

Back at Norman's place, he is putting on a dress and checking himself out in the mirror. Phil is in his own room with the door open.

Norman: I am really looking forward to this tomorrow.

Phil: If they only knew what was headed their way.

They meet in the kitchen.

Phil: Are you going looking like that?

Norman: What?

Phil: I assume you are going to shave tomorrow. And, you've got chest hair showing.

Norman: Yeah man. I'm not a woman. The idea is to freak them out and scare them into hiring me.

Phil: But you look like a slob.

Norman: You are not getting this. I can't and don't want to pretend I'm a woman. I <u>want</u> to look like a <u>guy</u> in a dress. If I go in looking normal, they will pretend that they don't know my approximate age and then they will decline me saying I'm "just not right for the job." This is the counter attack. They won't be able to pretend that they can't tell that I'm a guy in a dress and they will feel the threat of a potential discrimination lawsuit. And then they will hire me. That's the whole idea. I want to scare them into hiring me.

Phil smiles.

Phil: I think that may work. God speed.

CHAPTER 12

INTERVIEW DAY

The next morning, Norman is waiting for the bus, many people give him a second look but that's it. He gets on the bus and heads downtown.

He, of course, isn't used to wearing a dress, and even though it's more accepted in San Francisco it's an uncomfortable bus ride downtown. When he gets downtown, he finds the building, and makes his way to the reception desk. The receptionist is a cute girl in her low 20s and dressed in jeans and a t-shirt. Norman speaks in his normal man's voice.

Norman: Hi, I have an interview.

The receptionist's eyes open wide in shock but then she immediately compensates with a huge fake smile.

Norman: I'm supposed to ask for Heather.
Fatima: OK, I'll let her know you are here. Why don't you have a seat.
Norman: Thanks.

Fatima sends a text to Heather. "Norman is here for an interview. Be ready for a big surprise."

Norman sits down, looks at the magazines and reads one, sitting in a guy pose with his legs open. He is the only person in the waiting area. Heather comes out and looks at Fatima. Fatima points out Norman. Heather looks at him and has the same reaction as Fatima did. Suddenly she is very uncomfortable and stressed. She looks back at Fatima who has a big smile on her face, almost laughing knowing how Heather feels. Heather gets up the nerve to approach Norman and goes in with an air of confidence.

Heather: Hi, Norman?
Norman: Yeah.

Heather: I'm Heather. Nice to meet you.

Heather is nervously fake smiling thinking she doesn't want to touch this guy. But she puts her hand out to shake Norman's hand. He smiles, gets up and shakes her hand.

Norman: You too.
Heather: Come on back. It's a nice day isn't it?
Norman: Beautiful.

As they walk through the office, one or two people notice Norm. One is a guy named Chuck, who is noticeably gay and who locks eyes with Norman and gives him a big smile. Norman looks away and at that point realizes he must feel like women feel when they get unwanted looks. The dress transported him into another dimension.

Heather: Can I get you something to drink?
Norman: No thanks, I'm good.

Heather and Norman go into a conference room with a glass wall that borders the rest of the office space.

Heather: My boss Pete, the head of HR, should be along any minute. Oh here he is!

Pete does a double take and looks at Norman in a way not knowing how to react.

Heather: Pete this is Norman Desmond. He'll be interviewing for the Database Engineering position.

They shake hands. The understanding was Heather would be interviewing Norman but now that she sees him, she want's nothing of it.

Heather: I'll be at my office.

She walks out of the conference room and closes the door with Pete in there.

Pete: Norman Desmond?

Norman caught this guy's psychological slip that he showed surprised at Norman's name. All these thoughts came to mind in the next one second: In other words this guy hadn't read his resume and he didn't even know who he was talking to. In the phone interview, Heather had shown she didn't read the resume either. So Norman was thinking he was right, and they called him in here for practice and with no intent on hiring him. So wearing the dress was a good move. One thing didn't make sense though; the head of HR shouldn't need practice interviewing. But something was definitely up. Challenge on. Norman smiled.

Norman: Yeah, my parents were big fans of the movie Sunset Boulevard. They were going to name me Norma Desmond if I was a girl, but, I was a guy. Could they have named me after the male lead, Joe? No. They went with Norman.
Pete: Ha. Great story, great movie. Let me tell you about the company.

Across the office, the receptionist walks by and Chuck approaches her.

Chuck: Who is that?
Fatima: A database engineer.

Chuck: I know I'm in marketing but can I interview him?

Fatima: Haha.

Back in the conference room, the interview goes on. 20 minutes later:

Norman: ...so it was quite an intricate problem, but we figured it out.

Pete: Impressive. Tell you what, let me bring you right over to the engineering director.

Norman: Cool!

They go to the engineering director's office.

Pete: Diego, This is Norman Desmond. He's interviewing for a Database Engineering role.

Diego doesn't flinch like the others did. He couldn't care less about the dress.

Diego: Hi nice to meet you. Have a seat.

Diego closes the door. Pete walks away and goes to Heather's office.

Heather: You don't want me to interview him, do you?
Pete: Why bother.
Heather: So if there isn't a role, why bring in Diego?
Pete: I told Diego that we had someone coming in if he actually wanted to meet him. Diego likes to talk to people and know who is out there just in case something opens up.

An hour later. Diego walks Pete out to Heather.

Diego: Heather, we are all set. He knows his stuff. Nice to meet you Norman.
Norman: Hey, you too.

Diego shakes Norman's hand and leaves.

Heather: OK, great. I'll walk you out and we'll be in touch.

When Norman gets outside he makes a manly gesture like he made a good sports play.

Norman: Yes!

Someone walking by looks at him. H looks funny doing such a gesture in a dress. Back in the company offices, Pete and Heather are talking.

Pete: OK, what to do.
Heather: Diego said he knows his job.
Pete: Yeah, but come on. I'm wondering, if we don't hire him, could he sue us for discrimination? Let's ask the lawyer.

They walk over to the lawyer's office

Pete: Norman Desmond. Do you think that's his real name? Or is he a drag queen and he changed it to that?

They knock on the lawyer's door.

Craig: Come in.
Pete: Craig, got a minute?
Craig: Yup.

Craig is listening but he's typing something on his computer.

Pete: Out of curiosity, we just interviewed a guy in a dress.

Craig stops typing and looks at Pete.

Craig: You have my attention.
Pete: Are there laws we should know about for this situation?
Craig: You mean about hiring him?
Pete: Yes.
Craig: Define dress.
Pete: A very nice flowery sun dress.
Craig: Are you sure it's a guy?
Pete: Five day beard and a low voice.
Heather: And chest hair.

Heather looks slightly turned on. She got used to the idea of a guy in a dress. She just saw him for the guy he was.

Craig: Wow, he sounds like a real looker.

Pete remembers him sitting with his legs open not crossed.

Craig: How did he do in the interview?

Pete: Diego said he was good.

Craig: By the way, what is the job?

Pete: Database Engineer.

Craig: Outside of his appearance is he a freak?

Pete: Define freak.

Craig: Mentally unstable. Emotionally unstable.

Pete: No, he acted quite normal.

Craig: So he's just your average everyday transvestite.

Pete: Well, I don't know what average is, but, yeah, ok.

Craig: Hire him.

Pete: Could he sue us if we don't?

Craig: Yup. Hire him.

Pete: The thing is, this was supposed to be a practice interview.

Craig: What do you mean?

Pete: There isn't really a job. Heather is new and we called this guy in under the guise there was a job, but it was really just to give her practice interviewing.

The lawyer looks upset.

Craig: Well guess what? You screwed yourself. So now magically there is a job and you are hiring him.

Pete: Great.

Craig: For future reference, don't call people in for fake jobs and practice. They aren't lab rats. You thought you were going to take advantage of him but you didn't. You not only screwed yourself; you screwed the company too. You just cost this company the price of his salary, which I assume is six figures.

Pete: Yeah. How come I get the feeling we are being set up to be in a surprise reality tv show.

Craig: Yeah, that's funny. Pete, lets talk. Heather, you can go.

Heather leaves and the door closes. The lawyer doesn't look happy

CHAPTER 13

POST INTERVIEW

Norman gets home and changes into men's clothes.

Phil: How was the interview?

Norman: It went quite well.

Phil: Did they like the dress?

Norman: I think so. It was me that felt freaked out. Just a little. I'm taking Pavlov for a walk.

Norman puts on his regular clothes and takes Pavlov for a walk. He sees the beautiful runner this time cycling up a steep hill. A few minutes later his phone beeps. It's an **email from Heather**. It states: "*When can you start?*"

Norman: Yes!!!

That night, Norman goes on a date with Marianne to a nice casual Italian restaurant. She looks amazing. They are talking and laughing and there is magic in the air. There is a fly that they keep waving away. At one point the fly lands on Norman's ear. With lightning fast reflexes, Marianne grabs it, killing it.

Marianne: Got it. Pardon me while I go wash my hands.

She goes, washes her hands, comes back and the magic continues.

After dinner, Norman walks her home in the fog. When they get to her place:

Marianne: This was nice.
Norman: Yeah.

They have a great kiss at the door.

Marianne: Call me.

Norman: OK.

She goes to open the door and then turns back and engages another kiss, this time a bit more passionately. She lets out a slight moan and then breaks the kiss.

Marianne: Good night.

She goes inside and closes the door. Norman walks away in the fog.

CHAPTER 14

SHRINK THINK

The next day, Norman has his appointment at his psychiatrist's office.

Norman: I got a job!

Dr. Allen: Great! Doing what?

Norman: Database engineering.

Dr. Allen: Fantastic. You must be relieved.

Norman: You know it. It's kind of a funny story too.

Dr. Allen: Oh?

Norman: Yeah. I was so desperate for a job that I went into the interview wearing a dress.

There is a long pauses as the shrink looks at Norman.

Dr. Allen: Are you serious?

Norman: Yup!

Dr. Allen: Wouldn't you think wearing a dress would tip them onto the side of <u>not</u> giving you a job because, oh, I don't know, they might think you were crazy?

Norman: Yes, but that's the brilliant part. I really needed this job and I took a chance betting they would have to hire me for fear of getting a discrimination lawsuit.

Dr. Allen: Are you serious?

Norman: Yeah. Pretty smart, huh?

Dr. Allen: And how did you feel wearing the dress?

Norman: A little uncomfortable at first but then I got into the interview groove and just forgot about the dress.

Dr. Allen: Huh. What kind of dress?

Norman: A nice, tasteful, flowery sun dress.

Dr. Allen: Huh. Low cut?

Norman: Just a little.

Dr. Allen: Huh. Did you wear a bra?

Norman: No, I didn't fake it. Full chest hair showing.

Dr. Allen: Huh. High heels?

Norman: What are you kidding? Those things will kill you. I don't know how women walk in them.

Dr. Allen: Huh. Did you do your hair and nails?

Norman: No, in fact I went with a scruffy unshaven face.

Dr. Allen: Huh. So, just out of curiosity, did you notice if the people interviewing you had any discomfort or gave you any weird looks?

Norman thinks about it.

Norman: A little at first. But after that it was a very professional interview.

Dr. Allen: Professional. So how long have you owned dresses?

Norman: It's not like that. I bought one for the interview.

Dr. Allen: One.

Norman: Well, a few.

Dr. Allen: A few.

Norman: Well, I wanted to get some opinions and pick the best one.

Dr. Allen: Huh. So are you going to wear these dresses out?

Norman: What do you mean?

Dr. Allen: Like to the grocery store or to dinner with friends?

Norman: No. It was just for the interview.

Dr. Allen: Huh. And the job?

Norman: What do you mean?

Dr. Allen: You got the job under the premise that you wear dresses. You are going to have to wear dresses every day at work.

Norman: Oh shit.

CHAPTER 15

FIRST DAY AT THE NEW JOB

It's another beautiful day in San Francisco. The sun is rising, people are heading to work, some are getting off a ferry at the Ferry Building, some are on cable cars. Norman is getting ready for his first day of work. He is wearing jeans.

Phil: What, no dress?

Norman: I thought about it and I figured I would make them more comfortable and wear jeans.

Phil: Up to you but they hired a transvestite and if you are willing to risk the possibility that they think you tricked them, then go ahead and take that chance. they might fire you on your first day. So yeah. Wear jeans.

Norman: Shit.

Norman goes to his closet and yells to Phil:

Norman: By the way, I'm not a transvestite!
Phil: What do you call it?

He grabs a dress (which is the same dress he wore to the interview), puts it on and checks himself in the mirror.

Norman: A transvestite is a guy who likes to wear women's clothing. I don't like wearing women's clothing. I have to wear women's clothing.

Norman smells the armpits, nods his head like the smell is ok, puts on deodorant and heads to the door.

Phil: Isn't that the same dress you wore to the interview?
Norman: You noticed?
Phil: How could I forget? That was one of the funniest things I've ever seen in my life. Do you have another dress?
Norman: Yeah, but its not as nice.

Phil: That's OK. You already got the job.

Norman runs into his room and grabs one of the other dresses and throws it on. He again heads to the door.

Phil: Price tag.

Norman removes the price tag and hears a tear. He checks the dress and then he goes outside and walks to bus stop on the corner.

He sees a woman and she sees him and then she looks uncomfortably away. He gets a few strange looks on the bus too.

Norman arrives at the new job. Heather is at the front desk talking to the receptionist.

Norman: Good morning.
Heather: Well hello Norman. First day. Pretty exciting.
Norman: Yes it is.

Heather: Let's get you started on some paperwork. I'll introduce you to Carol, the head of HR.

Norman: Oh, I thought Pete was the head of HR.

Heather: He was. You caught him on his last day.

Norman: OK.

Norman smiles because he thinks his suspicions were right. Those being that his was a fake interview and then Pete got fired for it.

Norman: Oh, uh, where is the restroom?

Heather: Right over there. Actually, I guess I should ask, the men's room?

Norman: Yes. (he smiles)

Heather: Right over there.

Norman: Thanks. Be right back.

Norman walks into the men's room **thinking**: *This should be an experience.*

There are a few guys in the men's room and they are uncomfortable with Norman's presence.

Norman: Relax. Under the dress, I'm just a guy.

Norman goes to the urinal, thinks for a second about how to pee in a dress and then he pulls his dress up to pee. The other guys all leave.

Later that day, there is a department meeting with a room full of engineers and a white board that takes up a whole wall. The white board has software code and flow charts written all over it. Everyone in the room is in jeans except for Norman.

At lunch the women in the office are all eating salads. Norman is eating a meatball sub.

Woman 1: This is so good.
Woman 2: Same here. How's that sub Norman?
Norman: Fantastic.

A meatball squeezes out, falls on the plate and gets a little sauce on his dress.

Norman: Oh damnit.

He thinks about what to do. Then he pulls the soiled part of his dress up to his mouth and sucks the sauce off.

Woman 1: Norman!
Norman: What?

She gives him a few napkins.

Norman: Thanks.

He wipes the sauce off his dress with the napkins.

At the end of the day, Norman gets outside, says goodbye to a few co-workers and heads to the bus stop.

Norman's internal dialog: *Whew, that was not an easy day. And I'm going to need more dresses.*

Instead of going home, he goes back to the dress store.

Norman: Hi, do you have any more like this?
Eve: You mean with spaghetti sauce on them?

He picks out a few more outfits, pays for them and goes home. When he gets there, Phil is standing in the kitchen, beer in hand. Norman walks in the front door with bags from the dress store. Phil gives him a look.

Norman: What.
Phil: I can't wait to hear about your first day.
Norman: Actually it was good. Everyone was really nice to me. The men's room was a bit uncomfortable. But outside of that...
Phil: Cool. And how was it wearing a dress all day?
Norman: I got used to it. Of course, there are one or two women at the office who are so hot and let's just say my cover would have been blown if I stood up. I'm going to have to go buy a jock strap.
Phil: Anything else?

Norman: Yeah. You know, wearing this dress made me really respect women's cleavage. Cleavage is amazing. I just don't fill out the dress like they do.

Phil: Well, I'm guessing the dress designers had something else in mind. Try a stuffed bra.

Norman: Yeah right.

Phil: No really. Then you can try lipstick, heels, get your hair done. Really make yourself pretty.

CHAPTER 16

WEEKDAYS

The next day, Norman is on the way home from work, wearing a dress and he is thinking of his new girlfriend Marianne. He gets home and calls her. He is still in the dress.

Marianne: Hello.

Norman: Hi Marianne, it's Norman.

Marianne: Hi Norman.

Norman: I know its last minute but do you feel like doing something?

Marianne: Do you play tennis?

Norman: I have never played tennis.

Marianne: There are courts near me. Want to give it a try?

Norman: Sure. Do you have an extra racquet?

Marianne: Yes. Come on over.

Norman: Great. On the way.

Norman hangs up, takes off the dress and changes. Then he goes to Marianne's.

Marianne greets Norman at her door. She looks really sexy in her tennis outfit.

Norman: Wow.

Marianne: Thanks. So, you've never played?

Norman: Right.

Marianne: OK, let's go.

They walk down to the tennis courts near by.

Marianne: Do you know the rules or what the lines and boxes are for?

Norman: I think so but why don't you tell me.

Marianne: OK. So we stand on opposite sides of the net obviously, and on a diagonal. The serve has to land in the diagonal box. Then we hit the ball back and forth and for playing singles, we just have to keep it between these lines. The next point we move to the other diagonal and then the serve has to land in this box, and back and forth.

Norman: OK.

Marianne: These outside lines (she walks over to them) are for doubles matches. These inside lines are the borders for singles.

Norman: OK.

Marianne: But, we'll just hit the ball around today. No big deal.

Norman: Great.

Marianne is a much better tennis player than Norman is. She has fun playfully hitting the ball to wherever he isn't and watching him run a lot to get to the ball. After awhile:

Norman: How long have you been playing tennis?

Marianne: Since before I can remember. My dad wanted me to go pro.

Norman: OK. So let's see a pro serve.

Marianne hits a scorching fast serve that narrowly misses Norman. The fizzing sound of it racing towards him kind of scares Norman.

Norman: Whoa! OK, I'm done.

Marianne laughs, smiles, walks over to Norman and kisses him. They walk back to her place, walk inside, she immediately takes off her shirt, takes his hand and walks to her bedroom. They have really hot sex. Afterwards:

Norman: So, what are you doing this weekend?
Marianne: Nothing special. Got any ideas?
Norman: Want to go to a star party Saturday night?
Marianne: You know celebrities?
Norman: No, stars.

There is a pause as Marianne thinks, wondering what the difference between celebrities and stars is.

Norman: It's in Marin.

The next day, Norman is working at his desk (in a dress). People are starting to pack up and leave.

Employee 1: So long

Employee 2: Have a good weekend.

Chuck: Looking good sport.

Norman looks at the time on his computer and its 5pm. He heads home on a crowded bus wearing a dress. He gets home and collapses on the couch.

Phil: Tough day at work honey?

CHAPTER 17

STAR PARTY

It's Saturday. Norman showers and puts on guys clothes. Then he leaves and walks to Marianne's place. She lives in another neighborhood and he walks...up and down steep hills. She answers the door in a stunning dress.

Norman: Wow.

Marianne: Thanks. You look casual.

Norman: Yeah, it's not a dress up party. I'd say jeans, casual shirt and a jacket. It might get cold.

Marianne: Might get cold?

Norman: Yeah, it's outside on top of a mountain.

Marianne: OK…

Marianne was still thinking celebrities and dressing

up. So now she really doesn't know what kind of party Norman is talking about but she goes into her bedroom and changes. She assumes it's just a casual hang out with celebrities.

Norman: By the way…
Marianne: Yeah…
Norman: San Francisco is a walking town so I got rid of my car when I moved here. Do you have a car?

Marianne laughs.

Marianne: Now you ask?
Norman: Yeah, sometimes I don't think ahead.
Marianne: Yes, I have a car.

Marianne comes out in jeans, a black t-shirt and leather jacket.

Norman: Wow. Wow. Wow.

She smiles and they leave. We see them driving over the Golden Gate Bridge and up the winding roads to the top of the big mountain in Marin County, Mount

Tamalpais. It's sunset and the view is amazing. One can see San Francisco and the Bay. At the top, there are other cars there in a dirt parking area. There are also people there setting up telescopes. It's getting dark.

Marianne: What is this?

Norman: See the telescopes? It's a star party.

Marianne: Huh?

Norman: They do this once a month. In the city you can't see stars much but up here the city lights don't cause a problem.

Marianne: Oh! Stars!

After dark, people are lined up to see what's in the various telescopes. Norman and Marianne are in line to look in a telescope. They get to the front.

Marianne: What this pointed at?

Telescope Owner 1: Saturn.

Marianne looks.

Marianne: Oh wow! Wait, it moved out of view.

Telescope Owner 1: Oh. That's because Saturn is moving and the Earth is spinning. And because I forgot to turn on the tracker so it will follow Saturn. Hold on a second.

He presses a button to turn on the tracker and then looks in the telescope till he finds Saturn again.

Telescope Owner 1: There you go.
Marianne: Oh, this is so cool.

Norman looks after her and they go to another telescope.

Marianne: Whatcha got here?
Telescope Owner 2: Jupiter.

Marianne looks in the telescope and sees Jupiter and some dots around it.

Marianne: Wow. What are those dots around Jupiter?
Telescope Owner 2: Moons.
Marianne: What?! Seriously?
Telescope Owner 2: Yup. 4 of them?

Marianne: Yeah!

Norman: Jupiter actually has 95 moons. Those are the big ones.

Telescope Owner 2: Right

Marianne: Cool!

Norman looks next and then they go to another telescope.

Marianne: May I?

Telescope Owner 3: Absolutely.

Marianne: What is that?!

Telescope Owner 3: It's a globular cluster. A few hundred thousand stars in a small area bound in a group by gravity.

Marianne: A few hundred thousand?

Telescope Owner 3: Yeah. Incredible. Isn't it.

Marianne: Yeah!

Norman looks in the telescope.

Norman: Thanks.

Marianne: Thanks

They walk away and see a guy with people around him. He's pointing into the sky with a hand held laser pointer.

Marianne: What's that guy doing with the laser?
Norman: Do you see the faint white cloud above us?
Marianne: Yes.
Norman: That's not a cloud. It's the Milky Way Galaxy and he's pointing out parts of it.
Marianne: Geeze. It doesn't look like in photos I've seen.
Norman: Yeah, they have to keep the shutter open awhile to get that detail.

They walk over to the crowd and listen to the guy with the laser who points it to various parts of the galaxy and explains things about it. He points out the center of the galaxy, the arms of the spiral and some other parts that one wouldn't know just by looking at it…but they are all visible.

Eventually Marianne and Norman get back in her car

and head back to San Francisco. As they are driving back down the mountain:

Marianne: That was great.
Norman: Yeah.
Marianne: Thanks
Norman: You're welcome. Glad you have a car.

Later that night, Norman is sleeping at Marianne's. Marianne picks up her phone and texts her friend. "Inga, I'm going to have to cancel tomorrow. Spending the weekend with my guy." She puts the phone down, spoons Norman and goes to sleep.

Norman and Marianne spend the weekend together. They also take a scenic drive to the northern coast including a 20 mile long road that goes from the highway an hour north of San Francisco through miles of cow fields to the Point Reyes Lighthouse. The Point

Reyes Lighthouse is down a long set of stairs to the lighthouse which is on the edge of a cliff overlooking the Pacific Ocean. Its beautifully picturesque. They see whales swimming up the coast. On the way back from the lighthouse, Marianne pulls over the car to the side of the road in the cow fields and they have sex in the car.

CHAPTER 18

THE BIG SURPRISE

On Monday at 6am, Norman wakes up and gets dressed. Then Marianne wakes up.

Marianne: Leaving?
Norman: Yeah. I've got a lot to do today. (He kisses her). I'll talk to you soon.

She smiles. He leaves.

Norman goes home, walks in the front door, showers, shaves, eats breakfast, puts on deodorant and puts on a dress. At about 8am, he heads to the bus stop, gets on the next bus, finds a seat and starts doing stuff on his phone. A few stops later Marianne gets on the bus. Without noticing Norman, because he is wearing a dress, she sits down next to him, and in a minute looks over and notices it's Norman. The shock wave erupts.

Marianne: Oh my god.

He looks at her and is excited to see her and then remembers he is wearing a dress.

Norman: Oh. Oh no.
Marianne: What the hell is going on?

In a panic he says the first excuse that comes to mind, no matter how stupid it is.

Norman: It's for Halloween.
Marianne: It's July.
Norman: Oh right.

He is speechless.

Marianne: Fucking San Francisco. Why did I move here? (She starts to cry).
Norman: Oh, don't cry. This is not normal.

Marianne: I know!

Everyone on the bus looks to see what's going on.

Norman: No, there is a reason. It's a long story.
Marianne: What. Valentine's Day?

He's afraid of saying the real reason out loud in case anyone he works with is on the bus.

Norman: I kind of don't want to say surrounded by so many people.

He notices the bus is almost at his stop.

Norman: We are almost in the financial district. I don't have time to go into it all. Please trust me. Tell you what, let's have lunch and I will explain.
Marianne: Lunch? What are you fucking crazy? I'm not meeting you in public.
Norman: Yeah. Um. Ok. We'll talk after work. Normal clothes. When I tell you what's going on, you will laugh...
Marianne: Yeah, right.

Norman: No really.

A guy interrupts their conversation.

Passenger: Miss, is he bothering you?
Marianne: No. I know the big stupid idiot. Thanks.
Norman: I'll call you. Please trust me. It will all be ok. I promise.

Norman gets off the bus and runs into Greg, one of his friends from the dinner brainstorming session. Greg is shocked to see Norman wearing a dress.

Greg: Oh my god. You decided on prostitution?

One of Norman's co-workers walks by, looks over after hearing this and keeps walking.

Norman: Fuck.
Greg: When I said this at dinner I was just kidding.
Norman: Greg...
Greg: I didn't think it was this bad.
Norman: That's not what's going on.
Greg: I can't believe this.

Norman: Greg, it's OK. Really. I got a job.

Greg: You got a job? So what the hell are you doing (then whispers) wearing a dress?

Norman: It's a long story. I'll tell you about it later.

Norman is used to Greg hugging so Norman goes to give Greg a hug but Greg backs off quickly in fear.

Greg: Hey.

They part ways. Just then Chuck form the office walks up to Norman.

Chuck: Hi Norman. Nice dress. Friend of yours wouldn't hug you?

Norman: Uh yeah. He was just surprised to see me...

Chuck: Here, I will give you what you need.

Chuck hugs him and Norman stands there confused about what to do. His arms are at his side and in his mind he is praying: **"Oh Lord, please make this stop. Please. I'm begging you. This guy isn't letting go. Lord, what do you want from me? Whatever it is, I'll do. Just please, help. (Pause).**

Please. (Pause). God isn't helping and this guy isn't letting go. What am I going to do?"

People in the area are noticing the hug and he is noticing them. Norman pushes gently away.

Norman: Uh, thats enough.

Chuck: Hey, a couple guys I know are meeting in the Castro after work for a drink. Like to join us?

Norman: Uh, no. I like to keep my work and personal lives separate. Thanks.

Chuck: OK.

Norman: OK, well I'm going to get a coffee. See you later.

Chuck: Ciao.

Norman gets his coffee and goes to the office. He goes past Chuck's desk and Chuck smiles at him. Norman gets a knot in his stomach, gets to his desk and digs into his work.

At lunch, Norman goes to a local pub where it's busy with downtown tech people. He orders a burger and a water and watches a rugby match. He doesn't know the rules of rugby but he needs to clear his mind. The guy next to him at the bar is looking at him.

Norman texts Marianne: Marianne, I swear there is a good reason for this. I would tell you now but its detailed and really too much to go into over text.
Bar Patron: You don't look comfortable in that dress.
Norman: What is that, a pickup line?
Bar Patron: No, just an observation. Hey, this is San Francisco. We are accepting of what others want to do. But I get the feeling there's a good story here.

Norman ignores him. Marianne doesn't respond. When Norman finishes lunch, he looks at the phone and Marianne still hasn't responded

Norman goes back to the office and buries his head in his work. A few times he looks at his phone and Marianne still hasn't responded.

Eventually the work day ends. The downtown area is crowded. People are walking every which way, some catching cabs, riding cable cars and drinking in bars. The fog is rolling in through the Golden Gate Bridge, over various neighborhoods and blanketing the city. Norman goes outside and catches a cab.

Norman: Fillmore and Broadway.
Cab Driver: Yes Ma'am. Nice dress.
Norman: Thanks (sarcastically).
Cab Driver: It clashes with your 3 day beard though.

Norman gets to his apartment and changes into jeans, a regular shirt and a leather jacket. Then he leaves to go to Marianne's place.

When he gets there, he knocks on Marianne's door. She looks upset and suspicious but lets him in. He enters and she slams the door.

Marianne: What.

CHAPTER 19

THE REASONING

Thinking he knew how he would explain the dress, when it came to the moment, Norman was nervous. What made him mire nervous was that Marianne was so angry. Norman stood there speechless, thinking.

Marianne: Speak!

Norman: OK. A few things. To start off, I have to wear the dress.

Marianne: Have to?

Norman: Its a survival issue.

Marianne: Survival?

Norman: It's for my job.

Marianne: Your job is making you wear a dress? Your survival depends on you wearing a dress?

Norman: Kind of.

Marianne was angry. Now she is getting angrier.

Marianne: Get out.

Norman: No really. Please listen. I'm not gay. People see a guy in women's clothes and assume he is gay.

Marianne: Did I tell you I'm a black belt in Jujitsu? I'm 30 seconds from throwing you out.

Norman: I mean…

Marianne: Literally.

Norman: Just let me explain.

Marianne: If you aren't gay, I have to say, I have friends who are gay and this is really offensive and an insult to their way of life. It's not a joke.

Norman: No, it's not a joke and I'm not gay.

Marianne: So you are straight?

Norman: Right.

Marianne: So let's hear it.

Norman: OK, I had to do it, because of the job market and the tech industry.

Marianne: Huh?

Norman: This is what's happening in tech. Silicon Valley runs on venture capital money. The VCs invest in a bunch of companies doing the same thing and then they see who rises to the top. It's a competition.

The companies that get profitable fastest will either go public easier or get acquired faster and by larger companies and for more money. The slower ones disappear.

Marianne: So?…

Norman: So the VCs and the people running the startups want to hire people who work hard. And they see young people working hard but that's because young people emote more and have a youthful energy. Plus, who doesn't want to spend their days with a bunch of pretty people. But the thing is those mannerisms that make younger people look like they are working hard are in part because they are in a slight panic because <u>they don't know their jobs</u> and they are trying to learn things that older people already know. So the older people don't panic and they do their work more gracefully, not to mention they don't make mistakes nearly as much. And people running the companies can't watch everything that everyone is doing, but they see the emotion and think that shows more diligence and work ethic. And <u>there</u> is the problem. The emotion is just a façade. 20 somethings work hard but they make a lot of mistakes and to find and correct those mistakes, the companies waste a lot of time.

Marianne: You've got 15 seconds to get to the dress.

Norman: I'm getting there. So those piles of mistakes and confusion are costly to the companies because they essentially slow the company growth. And remember, the race to profitability is important. But the mistakes aren't calculated. So the founders and VCs turn a blind eye because they like seeing people working harder and figure, it's just a few mistakes, everyone makes mistakes, so what could it hurt? So they just keep hiring young people even though a staff of all young people actually hurts the company in the race against time...an important race. So this is why I have this problem.

Marianne: I understand about the race, but I still don't understand why you are wearing a dress!

Norman: Because, all the companies are hiring 99% 20 somethings. So people in their 40s have a huge problem finding work. You would think that with more experience, someone would be more sought after, but not in tech. So what was I supposed to do? Just give up? Should I just wait till I run out of money, can't pay rent, go live on the street and die in an alley because of age discrimination? I was just a few months from running out of money and ending up homeless.

Marianne: OK. That would have sucked. (pause) But the dress.

Norman: So when I finally got an in person interview I wanted to increase the odds of getting hired. So I wore a dress.

Marianne: I don't get it.

Norman: I know odds are they wouldn't hire me because of my age, given what happens in Silicon Valley. So I wore the dress taking the chance that they would feel they had to hire me for fear of a trans-gender discrimination lawsuit. I was desperate.

Marianne: So it worked. You got the job and now you have to keep wearing women's clothing.

Norman: Right. I don't know why I got the job. I like to think I got hired because I know my shit. Either way though, I did get the job.

Marianne finally smiles. She gets it.

Norman: You know, throughout history, older people were revered as being wise. And I'm not even old. I'm 41. Now companies don't care about wisdom, they just want youth. It's like they think it's a party, not a money making venture.

Marianne: Well, welcome to my world.

Norman: What do you mean?

Marianne: Do you know what women go through in the job market? We are more pleasant in our demeanor, so guys think we can't do the job. They hire us less and pay us less. It's total fucking bullshit.

Norman: Yeah, people are animals.

Marianne: They make decisions with a cave man mentality.

Norman: No argument here.

Marianne: So are you going to wear a dress every day?

Norman: Actually, most people there wear jeans, so I think I will start to mix it up.

Marianne: Will they be women's jeans?

Norman: Ha ha.

Marianne: How about a nice pair of Capri pants?

Norman: Here we go.

Marianne: No really. Let's diversify your wardrobe. Let's go shopping!

CHAPTER 20

SHOPPING EXCURSION

Norman and Marianne leave her place and take a cab to downtown. They get out in Union Square.

Norman: Where are we going?

Marianne: To a nice boutique I know.

Norman: No wait. We can't go there. They won't have men's dressing rooms and there could be a problem.

Marianne: How did you get the dresses you have?

Norman: It is a small place in a small neighborhood and I was there during a slow time of day.

Marianne: OK. Let's go to Bloomingdale's.

Norman: That's a high end store. I'm pretty sure they wont let me use the women's dressing room either.

Marianne: We'll pick up some items and you can take them back to the men's dressing room.

Norman: Oh. OK.

They walk into Bloomingdale's and hop on the escalator.

Marianne: I am so excited.
Norman: I'm just scared.
Marianne: Here we go. Capri pants!

They get to their floor and Marianne practically runs off. She is bouncing around energized, like a kid in a candy shop, looking at all the options for Norman to try on.

Marianne: Oh, I like these plaid ones. What size are you?
Norman: Are you kidding?
Marianne: Try these. Oh, and black. Love these. Here.
Sales Woman: Can I help you?
Marianne: We are looking for Capri pants for my friend here.

The sales woman looks at Norman. Then walks around him in examination .

Sales Woman: What size is he?
Marianne: Not sure yet.
Sales Woman: Just coming out?
Norman: Uh
Sales Woman: Congratulations.

Norman just makes an unhappy smirk. Marianne smiles.

Sales Woman: We'll just get a few sizes of each and you can try them on.

Norman is holding onto more and more clothes and when it gets to be too many, he just drapes them across his outstretched arms and women drop the additional clothes on the increasing pile.

Sales Woman: This would make a great top for these pants.
Marianne: Definitely.

They add a few tops to the pile.

Marianne: OK, which is the men's floor so we can try them on?
Sales Woman: Up two levels.

They get on the elevator and as they are going up, Marianne spots the makeup counter.

Marianne: After this, did you want to check out the makeup and perfume?
Norman: No!
Marianne: High heels?
Norman: Definitely not.

The men's salesperson lets them in to a large dressing room and Marianne goes in with Norman. He dumps the pile of clothes on the bench.

Marianne: OK. Strip.

The guy in the dressing room next door hears this and his interest in piqued. Norman feels like a dog who is being yelled at for doing something wrong. He takes his jeans off and tries on the Capri pants.

Norman: Yeow, these are tight.
Marianne: They are suppose to be. They accentuate your ass and hips.
Norman: Great (he says sarcastically). Got a few sizes larger?
Marianne: Try these.
Norman: Still a bit snug. No room for the boys.
Marianne: The boys. Be back in a minute.

Marianne leaves and Norman looks at himself in the mirror.

Norman: What has become of me?

Marianne quickly goes back to the other floor, finds a larger size and a few other items. Norman tries on the tops she previously picked out. Marianne runs back (including on the escalators), knocks on the dressing room door and he lets her in. She sees the women's tops that he has on.

Marianne: Oh, very nice. Try these.

He tries the new pants on.

Norman: OK, this fits.

Marianne: They look great. Here, I picked up a few more options. Try these.

Norman: Are you having fun?

Marianne: The time of my life. Unbutton your shirt more. Like this

Marianne unbuttons her shirt showing more cleavage.

Norman: Marianne, that looks fantastic but I don't have cleavage.

Marianne: (laughs) Oh right. Just a flat hairy chest.

She touches his chest and then unbuttons her shirt completely. She is wearing a laced push up bra.

Marianne: So you couldn't look like this.

The guy in the next dressing room hears their conversation. Marianne moves in towards Norman until she is pressing up against him.

Norman: No, You are too hot. I love your breasts.

They start kissing. The guy next door sees that the walls go all the way down to the the floor. He stands on his bench but the walls are too high for him to see over.

Guy in Dressing Room: Damn.

The guy's wife is standing at the dressing room entrance. She yells over to him.

Guy's Wife: Are you done yet?
Guy in Dressing Room: I'm working on it.

Norman and Marianne are having sex in their dressing room. They are trying to keep quiet but the occasional soft gasp or moan or grunt comes out. So does a slight banging noise. The guy in the dressing room next door hears them. Then his wife yells at him again.

Guy's wife: Well hurry up.
Guy in Dressing Room: Shut up!

A few minutes later, Norman and Marianne walk out of the dressing room. They both have disheveled hair and both of them have a post-sex glow.

Norman has a few of the clothing items in his hand. The guy in the next dressing room peeps his head out of his dressing room to see what they look like. He smiles and goes back in his dressing room.

Norman and Marianne go to the counter on the other floor to buy the items. The saleswoman who helped them notices they look disheveled. She can tell what happened. The corners of her mouth go up as she smiles and then rings them up.

Sales Woman: Have fun?

Norman looks at Marianne.

Norman and Marianne: Oh yeah.

CHAPTER 21

NORMAN GETS NOTICED

The next day, Norman is walking to work wearing plaid Capri pants, a black top and a nice leather jacket. He looks so good that one pedestrian (a guy) smiles as he passes him, checks him out from behind and then does a double take in confusion.

Later, Norman is sitting at his desk working on his computer (wearing Capri pants) and adjusting his groin as the pants are a bit tight.

Norman: (in his mind) *These things are too tight. Why did I do this?*

In general, this is a good day. Norman is getting along with people at work while wearing the tight Capri pants. They are accepting him.

There are other days when he is wearing various things. One day when he just wears jeans and looks like a non-transvestite guy. His co-workers are surprised.

A few days later, at the end of one day, while wearing a dress, Heather invites Norman out with people from work.

Heather: Hey Norman, we are all going to a tech social event. Come along and have some drinks with us.
Norman: Well, I don't drink.
Heather: That's OK. Come on, it will be fun.
Norman: OK.

They go to a hotel event room. There are lots of people drinking, socializing and having fun. There are also a few displays set up by companies sponsoring the event. Many people are checking out the companies with displays, but more are just hanging out drinking and talking. Norman, Heather and a few others are all in a group talking and laughing. At one point Heather and Chuck go to get a drink when a photographer goes up to them and asks about the guy in the dress that they are hanging out with.

Photographer: Who is that?

Heather: Oh, that's Norman Desmond. He works with us.

Photographer: Norman Desmond? Is that his real name?

Heather Yes sirree. It's from some sort of movie.

Photographer: Sunset Boulevard. What does he do?

Heather: He is a database engineer.

Photographer: Wow. The apparel oft proclaims the man.

Heather: What?

Photographer: It's from Hamlet. (Heather looks confused). You know. Shakespeare.

The photographer takes a picture of Norman.

CHAPTER 22

PUBLICITY AND CONSEQUENCES

Norman is at his desk working. Two blocks over, some guys at an investment bank are talking about dating. One slick looking guy, Donny, is bragging about recent dates.

Donny: …and she's a criminal attorney, which makes sense because on the ride home, she puts her hand in my crotch and practically attacked me in the car.

Investment Banker 2: Nice!

Investment Banker 3: Nice!

Investment Banker 2: Hey Donny, did I see you talking to that new girl in the break room?

Donny: Yeah, we hooked up her first day here.

Investment Banker 2: Nice.

Investment Banker 3: Nice.

Investment Banker 2: Things seem to be going your way.

Donny: Bow to the master boys. I'm going to go out and get a coffee. Talk to you later.

He leaves.

Back in Norman's office, a few co-workers go up to him at his desk.

Employee 3: Hey look Norman. You are a celebrity.

Norman: What are you talking about?

She shows him her phone screen on a website called "San Fran Out," an LGBT+ community. It has Norman's picture from the tech social event the other night, while he was wearing a dress. The headline over the photo and article is "Diversity in Tech."

Norman looks at it in horror. Without saying a word, he gets up and walks outside. He is shaking and clearly upset. Donny, the investment banker, sees

Norman from behind and can tell by his body language that he's upset but since the view is from behind, assumes it's a girl. Donny walks up to Norman and puts his hand on his shoulders.

Donny: You ok beautiful?

Then Norman looks at him pissed off and Donny realizes he's talking to another guy in a dress. Donny recoils with a shocked look on his face, pauses in confusion and then walks away.

Norman calls Phil.

Phil: Hello beautiful.
Norman: Phil, I've got trouble.
Phil: You mean the photo?
Norman: You saw the website?
Phil: Oh, it's not just one website. That photo has been re-posted all over the place. You are coming up in news links all over the world.
Norman: What?!!!
Phil: Dude, you are trending on Google.
Norman: Oh my god!

Phil: Congratulations buddy. You are out.

Norman: No I'm not.

Phil: Yes you are. This is great. I'm living with a celebrity.

As Norman walks down the sidewalk, talking on the phone in a dress and a few guys walk by and high five Norman. Norman reluctantly complies.

Norman: What am I gonna do?

Phil: Enjoy the ride?

Norman: Not funny.

Phil: Maybe ask for a raise.

Norman: This is not what I want to be famous for.

Norman hangs up. Then Donny, who has his coffee, crosses paths with him again.

Donny: You know, I'm kind of open minded. Why don't you take my card…

Norman: Get the hell away from me!!!

Donny scurries quickly away in fear.

Norman walks into a deli to get a sandwich and the guy behind the counter recognizes him.

Deli Worker: Hey man, saw your photo online. Way to go!
Norman: Uh, Thanks.

He hi-fives Norman who still isn't amused.

Deli Manager: Today's lunch is on us, Norman. Oh, let me get a picture.

The guy takes out his phone and points it a Norman.

Norman: Please don't.

The guy takes a photo of Norman.

Norman eventually gets his sandwich and sits at a table alone, in his dress, eating his sandwich.

After lunch, Norman gets back to the office and his phone rings. He does not recognize the number.

Norman: Hello?

City Employee: Norman Desmond?

Norman: Yes.

City Employee: Please hold for the Mayor.

Norman's eyes light up in fear.

Mayor: Hi Norman. This is San Francisco Mayor Roth.

Norman: Hi.

Mayor: We saw your photo online and I just think its great.

Norman: Uh, thanks.

Mayor: We are introducing a program to help increase integration of diversity candidates and we were hoping you could come to a public awareness event we are having and maybe even say a few words.

Norman sits in silent shock.

Mayor: Hello?

Norman: Uh yeah. I'm still here. Sorry, this whole thing has caught me by surprise.

Mayor: Hehe. And it's just great Norman. So is that a yes?

A co-worker walks up to Norman's desk while looking at the laptop computer that she's carrying, so she doesn't see that Norman is on the phone.

Employee 4: Uh, Norman?

Norman turns and sees his co-worker and responds to her:

Norman: Yes?

The mayor thinks the "yes" is Norman's acceptance.

Mayor: Great. My people will contact you with details.

The Mayor hangs up.

Norman: Uh, wait!

Norman puts his hands over his face in worry.

Norman: What am I gonna do?

Employee 4: I'll come back later.

Norman's phone beeps. It's a **text from Marianne** which reads "Sexy picture!"

CHAPTER 23

AND MORE CONSEQUENCES

The next day, Norman is at his psychiatrist's office.
He's lying on the couch all tensed up.

Dr. Allen: So I saw you on the 10 o'clock news.
Norman: Oh god.
Dr. Allen: You were wearing a very fetching dress.

Norman replies reluctantly.

Norman: Thanks.
Dr. Allen: So? How's the job?
Norman: Actually, the job was working out fine.
Dr. Allen: Was?
Norman: Well, it still is but now I am fricking famous.
Dr. Allen: Oh, a little bit of fame never hurt anyone.

Norman: No?

Dr. Allen: Well, it will come with a little stress.

Norman: A little.

Dr. Allen:...and an adjustment period.

Norman: Adjustment period.

Dr. Allen: But in time, I'm sure you will get used to being the most famous transvestite on Earth.

Norman: I'm not a transvestite.

Dr. Allen: Oh no?

There is a long pause.

Norman: What am I gonna do?

Dr. Allen: I don't know. But this was your choice.

Norman: I didn't choose fame. I just needed a job.

Dr. Allen: And now you are enjoying the spoils of war.

Norman: Spoils.

Dr. Allen: I quote William Shakespeare. "Be not afraid of greatness. Some are born great, some achieve greatness, and others have greatness thrust upon them."

Norman: You're not helping.

Dr. Allen: Listen, I know you didn't ask for this, but now it happened. Try to look forward and not back.

You can't go back. Maybe take these lemons and make lemonade.

Norman: How?

Dr. Allen: Well, take a page from Monica Lewinsky's book.

Norman: Monica Lewinsky?

Dr. Allen: If you are lucky, you will end up like her.

Norman: I don't recall her life being a bed of roses.

Dr. Allen: For a long time, it wasn't. Sure, she messed up but she was young and her boss was the one who let it go way too far. She didn't ask for fame and she had a long road back to anything close to normal, but now she gets national attention for anti-bullying and speaking out for human decency. Have you seen her speeches online? I'm quite impressed with her and how she turned it around to a positive.

After the session, Norman walks out of the psychiatrist's office and his phone rings. It's his mom.

Norman: Hi Mom.

Norman's Mom: Norman?

Norman: Yes mom.

Norman's Mom: Honey, I'm concerned. I saw something on the news.

Norman: Oh no.

Norman's Mom: There was a man in a dress that they said was you. Honey, do you wear women's clothing?

Norman's Dad: I told you if he moved to San Francisco, he would turn gay.

Norman: Mom, I'm not gay, not that it matters.

His mom tells the father:

Norman's Mom: He said he's not gay and it doesn't matter.

Norman's Dad: What?! Put him on the speaker.

She looks at all the stuff on the phone screen and slowly finds and presses the speaker button.

Norman's Dad: What do you mean it doesn't matter?

Norman: Dad, stop worrying about gay people. I mean, who cares. They are who they are. It's not your place to approve of them or anyone else for that matter. Just leave them alone.

Norman's Dad: Oh, you don't care?

Norman: No. And I'll tell you something else. Most of San Francisco is straight. We just respect the gay people. Do you know why?

Norman's Dad: Why?

Norman: Because they are people!

There is a long pause as Norman's dad realizes that Norman is right but he doesn't know how to win the argument. Then he tells Norman's mom:

Norman's Dad: Here, you talk to him. Tell him to come home.

Norman's Mom: Did you hear your father?

Norman: Yes and I'm not moving home. This is my home.

Then the father gets upset again.

Norman's Dad: Give me the phone.

Norman's Mom: Your father wants to talk to you.

The father takes the phone.

Norman's Dad: Son, I think your life has spiraled out of control. I mean, wearing dresses?

Norman's Mom: This is my fault. I should have worn pants every day.

Norman: Dad, its not what you think.

Norman's Dad: Just listen to me. I never told you this, but there were times in the military when you've been fighting and fearing for your life for a long time and all you've seen for months are men in the jungle. And things happen that no one talks about.

Norman: Dad, please stop.

Norman's Mom: What are we going to tell the neighbors?

Norman's Dad: Maybe we will just move. Start over. Become nomads. We can get by.

Norman: Dad!

Norman's Dad: We'll sell the house, buy an RV and move to Northern Canada where no one knows who we are. Tell us what we can do to help you son.

Norman: Stop panicking. It's not what you think. I just needed a job.

Norman's Dad: A job? So you gave up engineering to be a gay nightclub dancer?

Norman: What!

Norman's Dad: Son, we can help you. Oh, your mother is crying. I have to go. Think about moving home or stay with us in the RV. We can help you.

His dad hangs up and hugs the crying mom.

Norman gets home. He is about to walk into his apartment building when his phone rings.

Norman: Hello?

Miley Cyrus: Hi, is this Norman?

Norman: Yes.

Miley Cyrus: Hi Norman, we've never spoken. I had my agent track down your phone number.

Norman: Actually, your voice sounds familiar.

Miley Cyrus: This is Miley Cyrus.

There is a pause as Norman is surprised that she is calling him.

Miley Cyrus: Hello?

Norman: Uh, yeah, I'm here.

Miley Cyrus: I saw you've been getting a lot of press and I am very outspoken on this subject. Your story moved me so much, I just had to reach out to you and say, you go girl.

Suddenly the delight Norman felt is gone.

Norman: Uh.

Miley Cyrus: I'm sure this can be difficult in some ways; believe me I know how stressful sudden press can be. But I wanted to say, stay the course and don't let it get to you.

Norman: Uh.

Miley Cyrus: My friends and I are all behind you and we think its just great.

People in the room with her cheer. Some say "Go Norman!"

Norman: Uh.

Miley Cyrus: Just a little encouragement.

Norman: Thanks. Your agent looked me up?

Miley Cyrus: Yeah, they can find anyone. I think the agencies recruit agents from the CIA.

Norman: Ok. Yeah, I am surprised by all the media attention.

Miley Cyrus: I understand. Be strong. It will all be OK. Fight the good fight and know that we've got your back.

Norman: That's nice.

Miley Cyrus: Can I help in any way? Do you need any advice?

Norman: No thanks. I don't know what's going on.

Miley Cyrus: Yeah, it's a circus.

Norman: A circus, yes. Well thank you.

The people in the room are chanting: Norman! Norman! Norman!

Miley Cyrus: You're welcome. Take care.

She hangs up. Norman stands there stunned.

Norman walks in the front door. Pavlov is happy to see him and he understands why dogs are called "man's best friend."

Norman: Hi Pavlov. You need to go for a walk? OK, let me change. Ahhh, screw it. Phil, you here?
Phil: Yeah.
Norman: I'm taking Pavlov for a walk.
Phil: Thanks. Oh hey, a guy I know asked if you were single. What should I tell him?
Norman: Tell him I have a girlfriend and she thinks I look hot in a dress

Norman (still in the dress) takes the dog for a walk. A minute later the beautiful runner shows up. For the first time she stops.

Beautiful Runner: Hi!
Norman: Oh, Hi!
Beautiful Runner: Norman, right?
Norman: Yeah, how did you…

Then Norman realizes she saw the photo and is assuming he is gay.

Norman: …Oh right, the photo.

Beautiful Runner: Yes. Its great. I have to say, I had no idea. Every time I saw you, you were in jeans.

He contemplates telling her the truth but knows if word got out, he could have a lot of trouble.

Norman: Yeah well.

Beautiful Runner: You know what's funny? A week ago I was thinking of stopping and just asking you out. Boy would that have been embarrassing.

Norman stands there stunned and jaw open.

Beautiful Runner: Well hey, I'm Julia.

Norman: Hi Julia. Norman.

Beautiful Runner: Where did you get the dress by the way.

Norman: Oh. A place in Noe Valley.

Beautiful Runner: I like it.

Norman: Thanks.

Beautiful Runner: You know, if you want, I know a great guy I could introduce you to.

As if this day couldn't get any worse. Granted, he is happy with Marianne, but this woman has been his fantasy for so long and she just offered to send him on a gay date.

Norman: Oh! Uh, no, I'm all set.
Beautiful Runner: OK.

He again is torn whether to tell her what's actually going on, just to preserve the fantasy, but he realizes if his secret gets out, he could have serious trouble. Especially now that he's getting media attention. Although, he could just say he is bi.

Norman: You know, I'm seeing...
Beautiful Runner: Oh look at the time. I have to go. Got a hot date. I just met him today.

Norman feels like total crap knowing this fantasy is gone. He replies to her in a soft voice and looking at the ground in despair.

Norman: OK. It's great to finally talk to you though.

Beautiful Runner: You too.

She runs off. He watches her run away, out of his life and out of his fantasy. Then he talks to Pavlov.

Norman: (to the dog) Hot date. I guess I'll look at it this way: Marianne wouldn't have gone for a threesome anyway. I'm not that lucky.

The older couple that he talked to in Marina Green about age discrimination walks by.

Older Man: Oh good lord.

Older Woman: Don't tell me you did this to get job?

Older Man: This was your best idea?

Norman: Hey, it worked.

Older Man: Should we congratulate you?

Older Woman: At least it's a nice dress. Where do you get it?

Norman: A little shop in Noe Valley.

Older Man: You know what's great about getting old? Laughing at all the stupid shit young people do.

The older man laughs while there is a long pause as Norman stares off into space. Then the man pats Norman on his shoulder.

Older Man: OK. Have a nice day.
Older Woman: Bye.

They leave. Norman's phone rings. It's Marianne. After these last two interactions, he is not a happy camper. He answers her call sounding downtrodden but hoping she has something nice to say.

Norman: Hi Marianne.
Marianne: Hey, what are you doing?
Norman: Just walking my roommate's dog.
Marianne: Well, when you are done, want to come over?
Norman: Love to.
Marianne: And uh, wear the dress.

CHAPTER 24

LUCK

Norman shows up at Marianne's apartment. He knocks on the door and Marianne opens it.

Norman: You ordered a man in a dress?
Marianne: Yes I did. (She kisses him). C'mon in.

There is a very hot woman sitting on the couch with a snifter of brandy.

Marianne: Norman, this is my friend Inga. I hope you don't mind, she wanted to meet you.
Norman: Uh, no problem.
Inga: Hi.
Norman: Hi.
Inga: You were right Marianne. He is cute.

Marianne: I figured since you are all over the media, it would be ok. I mean it's not like I'm outing you.

Norman: Hey, why not. Did you tell her how this started?

Marianne: Yeah. We were just drinking some warm brandy. What would you like?

Norman: Well, the fog is rolling in. Got any hot chocolate?

Marianne: Yes I do. Instant ok?

Norman: That'll work.

He sits in a chair. Inga is at the couch and the two brandy glasses are on the coffee table next to each other. Inga laughs.

Norman: Whats so funny?

Inga: The dress.

Norman: I don't know how you women wear these. I have to wear shorts underneath them to feel comfortable.

Marianne: (from the other room) Good. Take it off.

Norman: Gladly. (He takes off the dress and is wearing shorts and a tank top).

Inga: Much nicer.

Norman: Thanks. So, I hear an accent. Where are you from Inga?

Inga: Northern Sweden.

Norman: Wow, I have wanted a long time to see the auroras.

Inga: They are amazing, but the winters are tough.

Norman: Yeah, not much sunlight.

Inga: And it's cold. We all stay in and cuddle up.

Norman: That doesn't sound like a bad way to spend a winter.

Inga: It gets you by.

Norman: How long have you known Marianne?

Inga: Oh many years. She was an exchange student in high school who spent some time in Sweden. We met then and have been close ever since.

Marianne: Inga moved to San Francisco about a year ago.

Norman: Oh really?

Marianne: She's a nurse at UCSF.

Norman: Great.

The microwave beeps

Norman: Plan on staying?

Inga: For awhile. Marianne has made it very comfortable for me to move here.

Marianne: Here you go.

Norman: Thanks. (he takes a sip). Oh, this is just what the doctor ordered.

Inga: Ha!

Marianne: How has your recent fame been Norman?

Norman: Overwhelming.

Inga: Is that a good thing?

Norman: I didn't like being falsely-"outed" but everyone seems to be OK with it.

Marianne: That's nice.

Norman: Oh and I got a call from Miley Cyrus today. And the Mayor.

Marianne: What!

Inga: Wow!

Norman: Yeah. She was really nice and he wants me to speak at a diversity event. In front of a crowd, on camera and everything.

Marianne: Wow!

Inga: Very impressive.

Norman: Well, its not like I asked for any of this. Someone took my photo and didn't ask. Then they just put me on a website without asking and it took off from there.

Marianne: Well, you seem to be handling it well.

Norman: I guess.

Long pause while they all drink.

Inga: I understand stress. Like I said, the winters, the move. My boss is always riding me. I don't know what I would do without Marianne.

Marianne: Awwww.

Inga: You have made my life here so much better.

Marianne: Well I love you.

Inga: I love you too.

They kiss. Norman is stunned.

Marianne: So I guess we are all outed today.

The women laugh.

Inga: Isn't she beautiful.

Norman: Very.

The women kiss again, but longer and more sensually. Inga looks at Norman.

Inga: You are handsome Norman.
Norman: Thanks.
Marianne: (to Norman) Are you OK?
Norman: Yes. In fact its a nice change from everything else today.
Marianne: Poor guy. Come here and let me give you a hug.

He moves over to the couch. Marianne stands up, kisses him and hugs him.

Inga: I want a hug.

Inga hugs him with her body firmly pressing against him. Then she kisses him.

Inga: I like him.

Marianne giggles. Then the women kiss again.

Marianne: I like the shorts.

Inga: I like the tank top.

Inga puts her hands on Norman's chest

Inga: Ooo he has a nice chest.

Marianne: Doesn't he?

Marianne starts unbuttoning Inga's shirt as the scene ends.

Early the next morning, Norman gets up and looks at the two women sleeping in the bed next to each other. He smiles as he gets dressed in his dress. Marianne wakes up and smiles at him. He kisses her. She goes back to sleep and he leaves.

As Norman is heading home, he has a song in his head "Walking on Sunshine." He is as happy as can be. He stands at the bus stop and when it arrives a big burly guy gets off and purposefully bumps into Norman.

Big Guy: Fag.

Norman looks concerned and a bit scared.

Big Guy: Don't look at me fag.
Norman: C'mon man. I don't want any trouble.
Big Guy: Then don't wear a dress fag.

The big guy reaches out to push Norman. Then Norman kicks him in the crotch as hard as he can. The guy falls to the ground, doubled over in pain and gasping for air. Norman quickly gets on the bus. The bus driver, who has been watching, shakes his head in affirmation at Norman.

Bus Rider: Wow, you kicked him so fricking hard. I've never seen anything like that.
Norman: He scared the hell out of me.

Norman is shaking as the bus drives off.

CHAPTER 25

WORK TALK

Norman gets home, showers, puts on jeans and grabs breakfast. When he gets to work, he is the talk of the office.

Employee 1: Hey Norman, I didn't get a chance to say congrats on the website yesterday.

Employee 3: Yeah dude. Way to go.

Norman: Thanks. I didn't ask for it and I can't believe how much press it got.

Employee 2: It's a good thing. Enjoy it.

The CEO's Assistant comes over to Norman's desk.

CEO's Assistant: Hi Norman. Mark said he would like a moment of your time. Do you have a few minutes?

Norman: For the CEO? Of course.

He gets to the CEO's office and Craig the lawyer is there too. Norman gets nervous.

Norman: So the CEO and the lawyer want to talk to me. If I jump out the window it's only 12 stories down.

They laugh.

Mark: No, it's all good. It's actually a congratulatory pep talk. Have a seat.

Craig: You've been getting a lot of press recently. That's great.

Mark: Let's be honest, since you are part of this company, we are also starting to get a lot of attention. Of course, this is great for us too.

Craig: We just wanted to ask what you were thinking of all this.

Norman: To be honest, I don't know. It all came out of nowhere. One day I'm hanging around with other employees after work; the next day people are telling me my photo was in the news.

Craig: Did you know the photographer who took your photo?

Norman: No. I didn't know my photo was even taken.

Craig: So they sort of outed you without your knowledge.

Norman: I guess so.. After that, I was instantly famous. I got some calls yesterday that surprised me.

Mark: Yes, the Mayor called us. He said you've been asked to speak at an event.

Norman: Yeah. And I have no idea what to say. I didn't even accept really, they misheard what I said on the phone. Now I kind of have to do it.

Mark: Well, we have PR people if you want some help.

Norman: Uh.

Mark: Thats their job really. You can talk to them about your thoughts and they can help you write it up.

Craig: Or they can go over what you write and help you fine tune it.

Mark: Or you can even go over it with Craig here.

Craig: Happy to.

Mark: No pressure Norman.

There is a pause as Norman IS feeling pressure.

Mark: You don't have to. We are just offering to help. Public speaking can be quite frightening if you aren't used to it.

Craig: I heard people are more afraid of public speaking than dying.

Mark: Yeah. Even if they are used to public speaking they are scared of it.

Craig: I read about some very famous actors who when they do Broadway, they get so nervous they sometimes vomit before the curtain goes up.

Mark: Could you imagine giving a speech or hosting at the Oscars? How many people watch that show?

Craig: I once gave a speech to a thousand lawyers at a conference. I was so nervous my knees were shaking and my voice was quivering.

Mark: Hey, but don't you be worried Norman. It's just a few quick remarks.

Craig: We are here if you want some help. Above all else, remember this. Preparation is key. Being prepared helps curb your anxiety.

Mark: Yes, and don't just prepare your speech. Get used to your surroundings. By that I mean get there early and take a slow walk around the area where you will be giving the speech. Sit in some of the seats. Stand in random places. Really get used to the area. It might sound dumb, but it helps.

Norman: Thanks.

Norman goes back to his desk and stares at the wall. Then he puts his elbows on the desk, his head in his hands and starts to mumble to himself.

Norman: A speech. What to say. Actors vomiting. We can write the speech. Time is running out. A thousand lawyers. Fear of death. Speaking at the Oscars. TV cameras. Holy crap. What am I going to do?

CHAPTER 26

GAME NIGHT CLARITY

That night, Norman gets home. He is still in jeans and also wearing sunglasses. He walks in to see another game night. This time they are all dressed up in medieval clothing and playing Dungeons & Dragons.

All: Awwwwww.

Norman: What. What's going on?

Sally: You aren't wearing a dress.

Sean: Go put one on for us.

Norman: Fuck you Sean.

They all laugh.

Phil: What's with the sunglasses?

Norman: People have been recognizing me. These help.

Phil: But it's dark out.

Norman: Yeah and I've been wandering the streets thinking.

Phil: About what?

Norman: About what to do about my speech.

Sally: Speech?

Larry: Speech?

Jeff: Speech?

Phil: What speech?

Norman: The Mayor of San Francisco called me and wants me to speak at a diversity event.

ALL: Whoa! Wow.

Norman: Yeah and I accidentally said I would do it.

Sean: Accidentally?

Norman: Yeah. Long story. So now I don't have the foggiest idea what to say. It's a good cause. It's just not my element.

Jeff: What do they mean by diversity?

Sally: A lot of companies exclude certain demographics from their hiring and it's illegal.

Norman: Like the age discrimination stuff I experience.

Sally: Right but more. They are supposed to hire a cross section of people in percentages similar to what actually exist in our society based on race, gender, religion, age, what have you.

Larry: Supposed to, but they don't.

Sally: Yes. But it's not just favoring white men. I've seen women owned businesses hire all women.

Alex: I worked for a Russian owned company once and 90% of their new employees were Russian. And they said they only wanted to hire Russians.

Alison: I went to an interview once for a pharmaceutical sales job and they asked me right to my face if I have kids. Totally illegal.

Norman: Most of the people at our company are in their 20s.

Sean: Then how did you get the job?

Norman: That's why I wore the dress in the first place. I figured they would pass when they saw my age. So I...I... wait. In my speech, I can bring up all these diversity categories but I can focus on the age thing. That's my demographic.

Sally: What do you mean?

Norman: I've been super stressed because I had no idea what to say, but I've been out of work for a long time because of age discrimination. Oh, and you know what else? Those fuckers at my job have mostly young people on staff. I was right. They wouldn't have hired me unless I checkmated them by wearing the dress.

Phil: I thought you knew that.

Norman: Well, I assumed it but I wasn't sure until now. Their whole fucking staff is too young, except two of the executives and the CEO is still in his 30s. If I didn't wear the dress, I would still be out of work and almost out of money. Oh, and they fired their HR head because of me. That asshole brought me in for a practice interview to train the young HR girl. He was never going to hire me. But once they saw me in a dress, they had to hire me and they fired the HR guy for setting up the situation.

Alex: Ha!

Larry: That's great!

Norman: You know what? I feel a lot better about wearing the dresses.

Larry: Glad we could help.

Norman: Oh by the way, please don't tell anyone I'm straight. If word gets out I could possibly get fired.

Phil: And given all this press and that now everyone knows who you are, you would never find another job again.

Norman sits on his front steps and calls his parents.

Norman's Mom: Hello? (she is sniffling)

Norman: Hi mom, it's Norman.

Norman's Mom: Oh hi honey.

Norman: Are you still crying?

Norman's Mom: Yes. I'm so sorry we did this to you.

Norman: Mom, you didn't do anything. I want to explain what's going on.

Norman's Mom: Yes we did. It's all our fault. We clearly made mistakes in how we raised you. I don't know what they were, but I will figure it out.

Norman: Mom, can you let me talk and just hear me out?

Norman's Mom: OK honey. I'm listening.

Norman: So you know I've been having trouble finding a job.

Norman's Mom: Uh huh.

Norman: So I've been out of work for a long time and when I finally got an interview, I didn't want to take any chances.

Norman's Mom: So you wore a dress?

Norman: Mom?

Norman's Mom: Go ahead.

Norman: So there are laws which protect certain groups of people from job discrimination and one of them is about transvestites. So I didn't want to take a chance so I wore a dress to the interview so they would feel like they had to hire me. That's all.

Norman's Mom: And the photo?

Norman: I was at a work thing. I didn't even know there was a photographer there.

Norman's Mom: Do you remember your uncle, Brian?

Norman: No

Norman's Mom: I'm not surprised. He was a great guy.

Norman: Was?

Norman's Mom: Yes. When you were little, he was

having the same problem. He was about 50 and he had been out of work for a very long time. He spun into a depression and he went to a very dark place.

Norman: What happened to him?

Norman's Mom: He eventually commuted suicide.

Norman: Oh my god.

Norman's Mom: Yes. It's such a shame. It was very tough on all of us too. The point here though is, this happens a lot. It's not right, but it happens a lot.

Norman: They have laws about it, but they don't seem to do enough and any process to correct can take years. Meanwhile people end up on the streets.

Norman's Mom: Or killing themselves.

Norman's Mom: Yes.

Norman's Mom: Well, I'm glad to hear you are ok.

Norman: Thanks mom.

Norman's Mom: Next time you are photographed wearing a dress, or whatever, please let us know before we see it in the news.

Norman: You got it.

CHAPTER 27

NORMAN'S LAWYER

A few days later, Norman is at a consultation he set up with an employment attorney. He wanted to know how to handle everything that's going on. He just spent 15 minutes telling the lawyer everything that led up to this point in time.

Lawyer: Anything else?

Norman: No. So what do you think?

Lawyer: You did the right thing.

Norman: Really?

Lawyer: Yes, in fact I think it's brilliant.

Norman: Really?!!

Lawyer: Oh yeah. You are absolutely on target in your assessment of the situation. There is a huge amount of age discrimination out there, especially in the tech industry, and it is so hard to prove in court standards. You practically need an email from the company stating they didn't hire you because of your age, but no one sends out letters like that.

Norman: Wow.

Lawyer: In the end, you took a chance and your strategy paid off. You probably did only get this job because they were scared you could sue them. Not only that, but they won't fire you due to this legal protection unless you screw up and cross the line in such an outrageous way that would make a jury full of nuns hate you. Like if you punch out the CEO. Being a transvestite is considered a protected class in the law.

Norman: But I'm not a transvestite.

Lawyer: Oh yes you are.

Norman: No, I'm not.

Lawyer: Are you a guy?

Norman: Yes.

Lawyer: Do you wear women's clothes?

Norman: Well, yeah but not because I enjoy it.

Lawyer: That doesn't matter. If you are a guy who wears women's clothes, then you are a transvestite and a protected legal class.

There is a pause as Norman feels sick and doesn't know what to say.

Lawyer: Congratulations.

CHAPTER 28

PUBLIC SPEAKING

The day of Norman's speech is here. He is outside San Francisco City Hall. There is a stage with balloons and lots of people cheering. Norman is wearing a sun dress.

Mayor: All too often our employment laws surrounding gender, race and other forms of discrimination, have been skirted, no pun intended.

(The crowd laughs).

The federal government needs to do more to tighten up these laws. In the mean time, we are introducing a program, including tax incentives for companies who devote a significant portion of their staff to be of diverse backgrounds. (The crowd cheers). Now I want to bring out a fine young person who has been in the public eye on this subject. Norman Desmond.

Norman: Thanks Mayor. I'm glad to see this program coming out. (The audience laughs). People need to work in this society and if they can do the job, then who cares what they wear or what color their skin is or who they want to sleep with <u>or how old they are</u> or any religion they practice? If they can do the job, then that's what counts.

The crowd cheers again.

Mayor: How about you tell everyone a little about you Norman.

Norman: OK. Beyond what you see, I have been a database engineer for over 20 years but as I got older, and had more experience, I got fewer and fewer interviews, never mind jobs. Age discrimination is real and it is big and no one talks about it. I got lucky and found this company that I'm with now; they are one of the few who don't discriminate

Craig, the lawyer, and HR people look at each other.

Norman: People over 30 now remove from their resumes older jobs and their college graduation dates to hide their age from companies who just want young people. To get around the age laws, these companies put on the job specs that they want someone with 2-5 years of experience, capping the experience IS age discrimination. And THEN those companies complain that they can't find good employees. Well sure they can, however they want someone with 12 years of experience but they hire people with 2 years of experience.

The Mayor's staff are making gestures to the Mayor to get Norman off the stage

.

Norman: Then to further compensate, those companies want to hire people from other countries who are under 30 ...and this doesn't have to happen. They just have to stop breaking the age discrimination laws... And the government has to have more forceful checks and penalties.

Mayor: What do you think of our program Norman?

Norman: This is a great program and it will help curb these practices. For centuries, the human race looked to older people for their wisdom. Now, if they make it to 60 they are rewarded with layoffs and then low wage humiliating jobs like working at convenience stores or fast food places.

Mayor: OK, all good points. Thank you Norman.

Norman understands that the mayor is telling him his speech is over. He leaves and finds Marianne is just off stage.

Norman: A bit too fire and brimstone?

Marianne: I thought you were just great. Needed to be said.

Marianne kisses him.

Norman: I saw the mayor while I was talking. He couldn't care less. He's a politician.

Marianne: They aren't interested in new ideas even if the ideas are ones that society needs. Politicians are just interested in marketing mass ideas so they can get re-elected.

Norman: Well, it needed to be put out there. Maybe he will like it by the next time he runs.

A reporter comes over.

Reporter: Hi. I'm with Planet Out.

He looks at Marianne.

Reporter: I, uh, thought you were gay, Norman.

Norman: Why would you think I'm not?

Reporter: OK. How did you get involved with this?

Norman: The Mayor asked me to speak after seeing me online.

Reporter: What do you think of this program?

Norman: It is much needed. All the discrimination going on is rampant and a big problem.

Reporter: You know the State legislature passed a law requiring diversity on company Boards.

Norman: Really? That's a great idea. More needs to be done but we are moving in the right direction.

Marianne holds onto Norman's hand.

Reporter: And if I may ask, who are you ma'am?

Marianne: I'm his good friend. Marianne.

Norman and Marianne walk off.

Norman: You know, on hot days, these dresses are really comfortable.

We see them leaving from behind. Norman scratches his butt.

THE END

About the Author

Jon Marcus is a Hollywood screenwriter who focuses on thoughtful comedies.

He went to The Ohio State University and got a BS in marketing after studying years of science classes and tutoring math. He does not have a degree in literature. He does not have an advanced degree. He did not go to an Ivy League school. He learned to write by watching a plethora of movies in an attempt to avoid his parents. He loves a good story and attributes his fondness of fiction and his sense of humor to a slightly warped mind molded by said parents. Not that he's complaining.

He is an enthusiast of science and history. He is also a romantic, not only of the way he sees the fairer sex but also in his vision of life. He has written numerous movie scripts, realized that people in Hollywood don't like to read, and he loves writing and creating thoughtful stories and fun characters. He also has a penchant for run-on sentences which he is working on and often tries to cure with commas and semicolons.

He grew up in New Jersey and eventually found his way to the West Coast. Currently, when he's not sitting alone in his dark Santa Monica home worrying about his weight, he can be found watching Pacific waves and playful dolphins from the Malibu coast and wondering what psychotic thoughts are going through the minds of seemingly normal looking people around him.